Approaches to Social Inequality and Difference

Series editors
Edvard Hviding
University of Bergen
Bergen, Norway

Synnøve Bendixsen
University of Bergen
Bergen, Norway

The book series contributes a wealth of new perspectives aiming to denaturalize ongoing social, economic and cultural trends such as the processes of 'crimigration' and racialization, fast-growing social-economic inequalities, depoliticization or technologization of policy, and simultaneously a politicization of difference. By treating naturalization simultaneously as a phenomenon in the world, and as a rudimentary analytical concept for further development and theoretical diversification, we identify a shared point of departure for all volumes in this series, in a search to analyze how difference is produced, governed and reconfigured in a rapidly changing world. By theorizing rich, globally comparative ethnographic materials on how racial/cultural/civilization differences are currently specified and naturalized, the series will throw new light on crucial links between differences, whether biologized and culturalized, and various forms of 'social inequality' that are produced in contemporary global social and political formations.

More information about this series at
http://www.springer.com/series/14775

Halvard Vike

Politics and Bureaucracy in the Norwegian Welfare State

An Anthropological Approach

Halvard Vike
University College of Southeast
  Norway
Porsgrunn, Norway

Approaches to Social Inequality and Difference
ISBN 978-3-319-87732-7   ISBN 978-3-319-64137-9   (eBook)
https://doi.org/10.1007/978-3-319-64137-9

Cover image: © Holger Hill/GettyImages
Cover design by Akihiro Nakayama

Printed on acid-free paper

This Palgrave Macmillan imprint is published by Springer Nature
The registered company is Springer International Publishing AG
The registered company address is: Gewerbestrasse 11, 6330 Cham, Switzerland

Acknowledgements

The current book draws on my ethnographic research in Norway carried out over a time span of almost three decades. My experience is that this research, involving participation and observation in a large number of political and bureaucratic settings have been very rewarding, not only in terms of getting access to relevant and interesting empirical material, but also at a more personal level. I have become involved in many interesting people who have been generous enough to open their worlds to me, very often even in situations where they could easily have kept me at a distance. To me, this seem to reflect a genuine sense of taking part in similar projects—trying to share experiences, interact, seek insight and develop knowledge for the sake of caring for the common good. Thus, I thank all those who have generously shared with me during my fieldwork project, without whom a book like this of course would have been unthinkable.

Numerous colleagues have greatly inspired my research and the ideas developed in this book. They are too many to list here, but it is of great importance to me to mention the intellectual environment in which I have been a part since 1990 (until 2014)—the Department of Anthropology, University of Oslo. Most of my work has been strongly inspired by colleagues there. Also, I want to thank the one person who more than anyone else has contributed to forming me as an anthropologist: David B. Kronenfeld. My wife and colleague Heidi Haukelien has provided invaluable inspiration and has been my main professional collaborator for more than two decades. Without her, I would not have been able to write this book.

Skien   Halvard Vike
20 August 2017

CONTENTS

CHAPTER 1

Setting the Stage: In and Out of Institutions

Introduction: The Problem and the Perspective

The present book explores how political mobilization from "below" may influence the distribution and dynamics of power in the context of a thoroughly bureaucratized, democratic state. The main case is Norway, but the larger Scandinavian context is also analyzed in some detail. My main objective is to try to understand the potential of horizontally organized social relations for cutting across and challenging hierarchical chains of command and centralization of political and bureaucratic power. This potential, I argue, is closely related to how motivations, identities, and social relations formed in contexts where social agents control largely informal resources that can be used to influence formal institutions, and to some extent shape them. The "institutional ecology" of the Norwegian welfare state, and the Scandinavian model more generally, seems to be characterized by a relative openness—or perhaps "institutional vulnerability" is a more apt expression—that to some extent has made it possible to prevent elite seizure of political and bureaucratic power. It seems to me that this phenomenon must play an important role in any attempt to explain how and why the welfare state emerged in the first place (Vike 2012, 2013; Stenius 2010).

In my perspective, two aspects stand out. First, political activity in local politics in Norway is heavily influenced by the morality and practice of membership commitment in formal organizations. As I show in this book, this seems to inspire an egalitarian social dynamic that imposes

© The Author(s) 2018   1
H. Vike, *Politics and Bureaucracy in the Norwegian Welfare State*,
Approaches to Social Inequality and Difference,
https://doi.org/10.1007/978-3-319-64137-9_1

limits on the autonomy of political and managerial elites, whose interests are very often driven by the felt need to seek to establish more and better control over what they tend to see as inefficient and/or unruly institutions. Second, the welfare state's universalist orientation, the idea that rights to entitlements and services are founded on citizenship rather than on some highly specific criteria implying extensive means testing (Kildal and Kuhnle 2005), seems to make it natural and easy to make strong and legitimate claims on "the state," and to challenge the autonomy and rationality of elites. Universalism contributes heavily to make public services "the heart of the state" (Fassin et al. 2013), and because so much of both political legitimacy and trust in public institutions depends on responsiveness to needs, the actual responsibility of public institutions is very hard to define and delimit. And, because public institutions, the municipalities in particular, "lack" clear-cut boundaries, they are relatively open and, consequently, accessible to many interests other than those of institutional elites that are supposed to control them from the top. At the same time, this logic seems to provide the local, democratically controlled institutions of the state—municipalities—with much more agenda-setting leverage than one would expect.

In sum, I call the unintended effects of these dynamics and conditions "the low center of gravity state," and argue that it is not some form of "Scandinavian" cultural disposition that generates such effects, but rather political mobilization and struggle of a particular type. By exploring such processes ethnographically within their proper social, cultural, and historical contexts, I seek to contribute to explaining why the Norwegian/Scandinavian version of the welfare state experiment has not (yet) collapsed. This endeavor has some analytical worth, as I see it, in the light of the fact that welfare states of the type that defined the utopian post-World War II horizon, and the vision of egalitarianism that formed part of it, today seems to be deemed unattractive, unrealistic, or impossible. The "low center of gravity state" metaphor seems appropriate insofar as it denotes both public institutions as centers of political gravity (Iversen and Soskice 2006), and the relatively decentralized and "messy" distribution of power within the institutional system. When the center of gravity is relatively low, maneuverability increases.

My perspective is anthropological, and does not focus primarily on how institutions ought to work according to some imaginary normative standard of rationality, but on how they are socially organized and work in ways that tend to differ distinctly from such standards. In order to map the social organization of the state, I have pursued an ethnographic strategy that I call "in and out of institutions," that is, collecting data across contextual and formal boundaries, following actors and the social relations they form across institutional contexts, moving up and down hierarchies, and exploring processes of decision making over time (Thelen et al. 2014). Another important element in this strategy is to explore institutional feedback, that is, the ways in which interpretations of the diverse and largely unintended effects of institutional action are conventionalized, authorized, and contested. Viewing institutions as emergent, contingent phenomena, I agree with Mary Douglas' statement in her influential book, *How Institutions Think* (1986):

> ...[It] is highly improbable that institutions could emerge smoothly from a gathering momentum of converging interests and an unspecified mixture of coercion and convention. We have too much experience of how easily they come apart and collapse. The thing to be explained is how institutions ever start to stabilize. (Douglas 1986: 111)

On the other hand, I am sceptical about other aspects of her sweeping, almost determinist generalizations, some of which seem to have had a significant influence in social science beyond anthropology:

> Institutions systematically direct individual memory and channel our perceptions into forms compatible with the relations they authorize.... Any problems we try to think about are automatically transformed into their own organizational problems. The solutions they proffer only come from the limited range of their experience. If the institution is one that depends on participation, it will reply to our frantic question: "More participation!" If it is one that depends on authority, it will only reply "More authority!" Institutions have the pathetic megalomania the computer whose whole vision of the world is its own program. (Ibid., 92)

I hope that in this book I am able to show why this perspective is unsatisfying. It portrays institutions as though they are formed by one single interest.

My perspective is also historical. Inasmuch as the institutional dynamics and properties I wish to uncover and describe emerge from forms of power struggles that over time generate specific sociocultural and political forms of contention, opposition, and identification, the analytical task of mapping continuities and discontinuities in institutional dynamics seems interesting and important. Many of the ethnographic descriptions in this book date back to the 1990s and 2000s, when I carried out several extensive fieldwork projects in Norwegian municipalities. These descriptions, and my analytical framing of them, can be seen as parts of an ongoing process of historical transformation in which the struggle to oppose the centralization of power meets new and more profound challenges. Finnish historian Henrik Stenius, in a comparative study of the role of associational life in political modernization on Norden, formulates a very fruitful question with regard to this transformation.

> To what extent did associational life – formally and semi-formally arranged horizontal deliberation among equals – substitute old vertical patriarchalism? And to what extent has a culture of everyday deliberation, fostered in the modern associational life, succeeded to defend democratic structures against the primitive forms of neo-liberalism and managerial authoritarianism? (Stenius 2010: 78)

ENTER ULEFOSS

In 1989/1990, I carried out fieldwork in Ulefoss, an industrial community of about 3500 people in southeast Norway (Vike 1991). Ulefoss has long industrial traditions, and economically it still relies heavily on the ironworks factory established in the first half of the seventeenth century. Until the 1970s, the community also included a vibrant lumber industry, illustrating Ulefoss' ideal location along the waterway, the Telemark Canal, running from the foot of the Hardanger Mountain plain down to the sea by the town of Skien (some 120 km southwest of the capital Oslo), on which timber from the interior of Telemark passed in huge quantities. Due to the influx of a large number of migrant workers and artisans taking part in the construction of the canal during the last decades of the nineteenth century, the community expanded considerably. This gave rise to intense political activity at a time vital for the constitution of modern Norway. Around the turn of the century, the labor movement grew very strong, comprising both a social democratic and a sizeable communist element. The main challenge for the movement was the nature of local industrial ownership, which was modeled on a highly paternalistic orientation and anchored in personal dependency.

During my fieldwork, aging members of the Labour Party in Ulefoss offered narratives of their lives and biographies that represented compressed versions of dramatic changes in modern Norwegian history. In interviews, I was presented with numerous illustrations of how people thought of the early twentieth century as a struggle against the form of power enforced by the owners of local industry: personal dependency. Until workers got organized and won the right to unionize, factory owners had more or less complete control over employees, and indirect control over the rest of the community. They could fire people by fiat. At the ironworks factory, the struggle for unionization was carried out very late—in the 1920s—but with remarkable success. The local struggle in Ulefoss was a part of a national mobilization that had already led the Labour movement into a leading position nationally, and thus people in Ulefoss had quite powerful outside allies, both in terms of labor market power and parliamentary influence.

The Norwegian Labour Party first rose to governmental power in 1928 (based on a revolutionary declaration, which made the experiment a short-lived one) and it established itself as the hegemonic political force from 1935 onward. The unionization struggle in Ulefoss ran parallel to a major change in housing standards and the local geography of power. Workers and their families had become able to buy their own land, build houses, move away from the factory owners' residential areas, and thus symbolically break away from their status as dependent labor. We may add to this, also, that the Second World War established a strong sense of national unity that in Ulefoss contributed heavily to transcending the fundamental experience of class as an imperative identity. This same experience of unity was further accentuated by the unparalleled increase in living standards taking place after the war.

A characteristic feature of the personal narratives I was presented with in interviews with older Labour Party members in Ulefoss was the strong working class identity, and support for the Labour movement and the Labour Party in particular. Being a member of the party was "natural," they emphasized; something that was both a precondition for a better society and a matter of belonging. Few of them spoke about ideology; they were much more concerned with how to act in unity. For Albert, a former ironworks worker who was 72 years old at the time I interviewed him, some basic experiences had shaped his sense of belonging in profound ways. The hardship imposed upon people in Ulefoss in the twenties and thirties constituted his primary point of reference. Many of his coworkers were unemployed, and he witnessed a deep anxiety growing in the community. In light of this experience, two significant political changes came to play an important part of his life ever since: the unionization of local industrial workers, and the rise to parliamentary power by the Labour Party.

According to Albert, unionization was important because it gave the workers the possibility to negotiate with the local employer "on the basis of law," as he put it. In this way, their powerlessness and personal dependence could be radically reduced and give way to a greater degree of autonomy and freedom. The success of the Labour Party in the national arena also created many new possibilities. For Albert, as a young worker, the Party's message, most importantly the slogan, "Jobs for Everyone," was extremely persuasive. He felt that it was directed to him and his kind. Being an active member of the Labour Party involved taking part in the collective struggle to provide "better conditions" for all, he emphasized. The leaders of the Labour movement were easy to identify with, because one knew that "they were to be trusted." Albert lost his mother when he was quite young, and the rest of the family depended heavily upon the support provided by fellow workers and their families. Most people experienced similar hardships, and had very similar notions of how things could be improved. For Albert, it was only natural that almost everyone he knew turned enthusiastically to the Labour Party.

Albert joined the union of industrial workers in 1935. In the interview, he thought back on this period as a particularly tough one. In light of the local employer's measures aiming to divide and rule and prevent unionization, the union leaders' radical attitude impressed him greatly, but made him somewhat anxious, too. He recalled several "wild and illegal strikes." He also recalled that things actually calmed down fairly soon. Not only were the factory owners made subject to law, the union radicals soon turned more moderate: their need to "show off" became less urgent. Albert identified with this moderation.

When commenting on the situation after the Second World War, Albert stressed that he happily observed that "things were levelled out." At the time of my fieldwork, he followed local politics very closely, and although he didn't attend meetings very often, he was active in informal networks of Labour Party members. He was deeply sceptical towards the leaders of the Party because, like many others, he felt that they were not sufficiently sensitive to "people's opinion." "They hardly deserve the trust that has been given to them", he emphasized.

When interviewing representatives of this pioneer generation in Ulefoss, I was left with the impression that they attributed the extreme improvement in their own and their children's lives to the struggle they had been through. The moral backbone of their lives was the idea of *standing together*. On almost all occasions when political interests were at stake, even in seemingly trivial discussions on local matters, breaks in the norm of standing together in Party votes were considered deeply immoral. The Party was to have but *one opinion* on all-important issues, most of my informants among the old guard emphasized. In the Municipal Assembly, all Labour Party representatives were exposed to a heavy pressure, formal and moral, to stand by the majority decisions made by the Party meeting that was always held prior to the meeting in the Assembly. Labour Party members had little respect for the political outlook of the local educated elite (which, during my fieldwork, were largely associated with the Socialist Party), who put a premium on personal opinion at the cost of the collective.

In recurring narratives, interpreting their own biographies within the larger frame of the remarkable socioeconomic changes that took place in Norwegian society in the twentieth century, the old Labour Party members in Ulefoss associated societal progress with the Party, its program, and their own influence upon it. For people in Ulefoss, as in many other parts of Norway, the emergence of the Social Democratic state was experienced as vital to the success of the local political struggle. The relationship between the local struggle, party membership, national identity, progress, and improved life conditions was perceived as very direct. And in many cases it appeared that in times of local conflicts, much of this cluster of historical experience was reminiscent of, and used as a moral metanarrative for current political discourse. Historical experience had confirmed that standing together constituted the basic prerequisite for political influence and desirable outcomes. Moreover, in order to stand together, the collective control of those representing the party in decision-making fora was considered absolutely necessary. In Ulefoss, this control was of a formal kind—for example, as noted above, through binding representatives to specific decisions made in the Party meeting—but also social and moral. Party members and their local networks would actively monitor the behavior of those representing them in a variety of arenas, and use the information gathered in this way to discuss the trustworthiness of political leaders, that is, whether they, too, would be willing to sacrifice their self-interest for the common good and respect the morality of standing together.

As political ideals, categories such as *standing together*, *common sense*, and *equality* were seen not only, and perhaps not even primarily, as the preferred outcome of policy, but rather as preferred properties of the decision-making process itself, the way in which the Party collective was supposed to reach consensus. In Ulefoss, *common sense* denoted a moral obligation to listen to and respect "the silent majority," those who did not possess expert knowledge but who often used informal arenas to deliberate and reach a shared view in political issues. In formal meetings in the Labour Party, they had a much more important role to play in Party votes than their role in debates would indicate. *Equality* referred to what I choose to call the morality of membership, which most often expressed itself as a critique of any kind of social distinction based on formal education, sophisticated speech, and the like. The informal procedures through which trust networks between equals were constituted and upheld, were articulated by the idea of *the majority*. This informally recognized idea of majority was mobilized as a means to control the formal power of political leaders whenever the latter was considered at odds with the general attitude among members. In Party meetings, it very often became a question of how to deal with the mayor (representing the Labour Party), when he time and again failed to understand what it meant when Party members tried to tell him that what he did was against the opinion of the *people*. In such contexts, *people* served as a rhetorical denotation of *the majority*. For them (those who portrayed themselves as the *people* and *the majority*) it was clear that the mayor's power was attributable to his tendency to dominate formal meetings and thus misuse the loyalty of members by overrunning their sense of solidarity with *the majority*. The effect was that he generated the sense among many that he did not "really listen." Interestingly, over time the mayor and his allies had to pay a price; he was not nominated for a third term in office.

During my fieldwork, an intense political controversy developed around a new plan for the reorganization of elder care (Vike 1991, 1997). The mayor and other leading politicians had led a planning process that concluded there was a need for a reform that would channel resources from elder care institutions to more "open solutions," providing greater care in the home. The basic idea was that this would improve the quality of care and enable the frail elderly to live longer in their own homes, thereby lessening the financial burden of the

municipality involved in maintaining costly institutions. In the beginning, there seemed a broad consensus that this was a good strategy, and
the leading politicians understood this as a "go" signal. However, after
a while, the opposition gained ground and became serious. The mayor,
who took the lead in fronting the plan, argued that his own party, as
well as the municipal health and welfare committee, had already com-
mitted to the plan and could not reverse the process. The opposition,
which consisted of several backbenchers in his own party and a considerable number of party members, as well as parts of their networks in local
voluntary associations, was provoked by the mayor's conclusion that no
further discussion was necessary and stirred to angry protest. Probably
as an attempt to bypass the growing opposition in the Labour Party, the
mayor and the municipal administrative leaders decided to arrange public
meetings to enlighten people. They largely ended up as failures. The one
meeting I attended got completely out of hand, and both the leading
politicians and the attending bureaucrats were almost literally thrown out
of the building and accused of being arrogant. The conflict kept escalating further for a while, but after a couple of months, a compromise was
achieved. Most elements in the plan were kept, but the transition from
institutional to home-based care was to be slower and less radical. At a
later stage in the process, when local political leadership was on the Party
agenda, the local informal party network had effectively disqualified the
mayor.

RECIPROCITY IN POLITICS

Marcel Mauss, in his legendary work, *The Gift* (1954), defines gift giving as the obligation to give, receive, and reciprocate. Through this
simple formula, Mauss investigated how social relationships and complex systems emerge from reciprocal acts and commitments. For Mauss,
and a large number of scholars after him, the gift serves as a highly useful analytical metaphor. It refers to a phenomenon that may be directly
observed; it depicts a specific motivation (or set of motivations) for
human beings involved in social relationships, and it points at easily
detectable aspects of the dynamics and interdependencies of commitments and the social relations emerging from them. Also, we may add,
thinking metaphorically of social processes as sequences of gift giving
may help us understand how individuals get caught up in larger institutional contexts in which social relations are organized by specific

combinations of formal and informal types of exchange. What strikes me as interesting in the Ulefoss case is the great emphasis people tend to put on social relations mediated by formal rules, and on moral conventions related to and made possible by such rules. Albert's possibility for exerting influence, as he saw it, rested on his membership in the Party and the union, and on the way he could take part in forging a robust majority that local political leaders had to respect unless they were ready to face moral sanctions (in the form of a bad reputation in the wider community). As representatives, these elites were subject to forms of control that regulated what kinds of "gifts" could be presented to whom, when, and how. Above all, the mayor seemed to fail to realize that in his position, his access to the formal, municipal administrative hierarchy was not of the same moral order as the mutual commitments among party members. They belonged to separate moral spheres, and party members guarded the boundary between them. Each member's autonomy was paramount, and in order to protect it moral pressure was directed at political representatives who worked closely with administrative elites and who could be tempted to believe that they could demand loyalty according to the logics of the administrative chain of command.

Equally important was the protection of individual autonomy from the influence of differences in status, wealth, and prestige. Within these moral boundaries, gifts exchanged between members tended to conform to an overarching, general moral principle: gift giving was mostly about coalition building, which took the form of an emergent process of supporting chains of arguments in the making. The recognition of a good argument and the expression of support thus served as prototypical gifts. Over time, the identification of good arguments tends to become associated with members with high credibility. In practice this credibility involves the ability to guard one's autonomy vis-à-vis leaders, a record for sacrificing self-interest for the common good (taking responsibility, showing up at meetings, standing a fight, etc.), and respecting the autonomy of others (involving, most importantly, refraining from assuming that the building of new coalitions may draw on solidarity established in previous ones). However, respecting autonomy meant that mutual support in coalition building was specific to each individual issue, so the expression of this respect involved acknowledging that the support of others could never be expected to build on previous exchanges. In moral terms, membership status introduced an element of equality that partly undermined the relevance of social status. Credibility and trust were seen as depending on the strength of one's commitment rather than education, talent, personal status, and so on. However, the relationship between the formal and the informal was clearly asymmetrical. Formal rules and procedures served as a medium through which informal aspects of the relationship between members had to pass and be sanctioned. At the same time, formal status (membership) and decision-making procedures always served as decisive reference points for the activation of informal resources.

Mike Savage, in *The Popularity of Bureaucracy: Involvement in Voluntary Associations* (2005), makes the point that social relationships of the kind we call "bureaucratic" are not only developed and cultivated by the apparatuses of the state. In England,

> All manner of people have enthusiastically supported and nurtured bureaucracies, such as trade unions, charities, sports, or hobby clubs. Bureaucracy has historically had strong roots in popular culture. (Savage 2005: 310)

> Indeed, it can be argued that the (no doubt partial) democratization of British social relationships from the early nineteenth century rested on popular bureaucratization as a means of resisting and countering elite patronage. (ibid., 313)

This perspective resonates with some of Max Weber's insights into the nature of modern bureaucratic forms. It carries a democratic potential in that it allows for the separation of social status from bureaucratic function, and bases itself on educational merit and professional ethos. The office is not supposed to be an extension of social position, and may in principle become independent from social class. Mike Savage's point resonates well with the ambition of most of my working-class Ulefoss informants. They clearly saw that the formal system of roles and procedures in unions and municipal politics provided them with tools with which their sense of collective morality could be channeled into political influence and break with the tradition of personal dependency that had dominated them. Not only that: Albert, for instance, clearly realized that the power of the collective morality as he saw it was important to nurture for political means resting on his own personal autonomy. Working-class members of the Ulefoss Labour Party hated the idea of becoming dependent on the formal power of the mayor and his allies, or other party members imbued with representative functions. The bureaucratic formalities characterizing the Labour Party and the municipal political arenas in Ulefoss became a set of (more or less) transparent rules for negotiating political interest. They provided a social infrastructure for a specific form of reciprocity. In order to be accepted as a legitimate member of the collectivity, individuals had to conform to the moral code of "standing together," which most often involved symbolic confirmations of being equal qua members, respecting the majority view, and actively taking part in creating consensus. "The politics of recognition" thus consisted in granting respect to those who held the overall aim of "standing together" in esteem, particularly those serving representative functions and offices. It also consisted in a symbolism of voluntary commitment, sharply contrasted with loyalty and social debt. On this basis, trust could be accumulated. The morality of membership was thus not mainly about denying inequality, but preventing it from being converted to individual political capital beyond the control of the collective of members. Everyone seemed to agree, in principle, which elected representatives should not be allowed to achieve any kind of autonomy in the sense of becoming able to maneuver independently of the continuous control of the membership collective.

In Ulefoss I observed many people who in political terms accumulated much "extra" respect and prestige by making an extraordinary effort; most of them did so by holding key positions in local voluntary associations. Their success relied on their ability to display a will to invest time and skills in building common goods, and, perhaps most notably, in never indicating that they were aware of the fact that the respect thus gained could be converted to forms of capital relevant in the political realm. In local politics in Ulefoss, no gift seems more valuable than receiving recognition for making an extra effort for the common good, and for not claiming status and weight beyond one's status as an "ordinary member." One of my Ulefoss informants, a well-educated man in his early forties working as a director of a regional housing cooperative organization, invested much time in participating in the Labour Party. At one point, he let some of his fellow members know that he would be happy to take up a leadership position, as he figured that seeking power is the very essence of politics. This explicitly expressed ambition effectively disqualified him for any such position.

The very simple logic of the gift gives rise to complex social systems far beyond the intentions and consciousness of those involved in single acts of gift giving. This seems to be what Mary Douglas has in mind when discussing *"How Institutions Think"* (1987). Institutions, that is, systems of conventions regulating statuses, roles, procedures, and relationships within a given social field related to a set of more or less delineated tasks, tend to relieve us of some of the cognitive labor of seeking adequate ways to behave vis-à-vis our fellow men. They do this by providing us with conventions and/or traditions that generate identification and recognizable context, as well as ways of regulating and interpreting the consequences of our own actions as they generate complex patterns. Institutions tend to provide conventional interpretations, or cultural models, in David Kronenfeld's terms (2008), of, and solutions to, challenges, new or old.

Gift giving is all about reciprocity, and reciprocity may place partners in social interaction on more or less asymmetrical positions vis-à-vis each other. The ultimate version of asymmetry is personal dependency, which constitutes a major element in the social infrastructure in most societies. In this book, I am primarily interested in social relations that follow a more egalitarian logic. Because egalitarian social patterns are extremely rare in contexts more or less controlled by large bureaucratic institutions of the state, I want to explore social mechanisms that allow for reducing or eliminating personal dependency. In gift-giving terms, egalitarianism and individual autonomy rest on the possibility to make choices as to how and when to reciprocate, as well as on the ability to withdraw from other people's claims, or possess the power to insist that these claims must be negotiated. In one important sense, this runs counter to Mauss' definition of the gift as in part an obligation to reciprocate.

My argument here is that we need a deeper understanding of how the right to withdraw or re-negotiate claims made by actors placed at some higher level of some administrative or political hierarchy becomes a part of formal organizational contexts, which dominate most aspects of all state-organized societies. Bureaucratic systems of command threaten to appropriate and undermine egalitarian horizontal alliances. One of the observations that stimulated my interest in this phenomenon as it unfolded in Ulefoss, was that the egalitarian logic of membership also dominated municipal decision-making arenas and, by virtue of that, heavily influenced the municipal bureaucracy as well. At the time of my fieldwork, the municipal bureaucracy was in the process of taking a more managerial shape, which involved an increasing accumulation of power on the part of administrative elites. Administrative claims on the loyalty of politicians in issues related to, for example, budgets and procedures, and tended to manifest themselves in relation to the implementation of state policy. As in the above case involving the mayor, such claims were most often mediated through the system of political representation, inspiring political leaders to achieve greater autonomy on their part. They sought to increase this autonomy by trying to claim loyalty from their fellows with reference to administrative procedures. However, in Ulefoss this proved very hard to achieve. The community was too transparent, and the social control mechanisms involved in the morality of membership seemed too efficient.

TRADITIONAL OR MODERN?

In theories of modernization and democratization, it is claimed that citizenship is anchored in individual freedom and autonomy, which in turn is a precondition for democracy (Parsons 1964; Wolf 1966; Graubard 1986; Friedmann 1987; Alexander 1988; Piattoni 2001). Therefore, modernization theory explains how the conditions of individual freedom are supposed to evolve from a traditional order characterized by personal dependency and nondemocratic forms of power to a "modern" one in which "all men are equal." When such equality is lacking, it is assumed to be a product of insufficient modernization and the prevalence of "traditional" structures that are still alive and kicking, such as in South European or Latin American clientelism and patrimonialism. Yet we know very well that relations of personal dependency are vital in most modern institutions of the state, as well as in the family and civil society throughout the West and elsewhere. As Randall Collins (2011) has pointed out,

> In Max Weber's grand historical panorama of the transition from medieval to modern societies, one can make out a good case that the key feature on the organizational level has been the shift from patrimonialism to bureaucracy. But the shift has never been completely successful, and the bad dreams as well as the romances of modernity often take the form of a resurgent patrimonialism (p. 16).... Patrimonialism wields political power in the form of personal loyalty and arbitrary discretion, tempered only by tradition (p. 17).... Patrimonial organization is an enduring possibility that reemerges spontaneously whenever bureaucracy is resisted or breaks down from its own debilities (p. 21).

In the anthropology and sociology of democratic change in Europe, a particular fascination for the transformation of the role of kinship in politics has long prevailed (Wolf 1966; Brøgger 1990; Herzfeld 1992; Papakostas 2001; Roniger 1998). For example, how and when are corporate kin-groups marginalized, transformed, or substituted by the logics of democratic mass politics, market relations, and universal bureaucratic procedures, all of which—according to the ideal type—individualize social relations and form class relations upon them? Erik Wolf, in his classic study of rural transformation in the Swiss Alps in the 1950s (Wolf 1966), points out that modern political institutions never seem to become independent of what he calls "supplementary interpersonal sets," meaning corporate groups tied together by some kind of traditional deeper loyalty. This "hidden mechanism of complex society" (the interpersonal sets) may explain, for example, how behavioral forms spread in society. Wolf refers to the generalization and downward spread of public school manners in Britain and courtly forms in France, as well as the upward spread of the behavioral etiquette of a despised interstitial group in Mexico which became the grammar standardization between powerholders and followers (ibid., 20). Formal institutions are always based on informal social systems in some way or another, and, accordingly, on the metaphorical images, ideals as well as nostalgic collective memories they objectify. This may have very little to do with kinship and its significance for the maintenance of collective resources and forms of loyalty in local communities; it may, for example, reappear as particular forms of patronage and clientelism among elite groups. In this perspective, the distinction between the modern and the traditional appears rather blurred and perhaps even conceptually meaningless. In Ulefoss, the organizational forms dominating local politics involved ways of regulating social relationships that can be seen closer to the category of "the modern" than the more "traditional" forms of personal loyalty introduced through administrative managerialism. They constituted, in Wolf's terms, behavioral forms that had spread "upwards."

If we are to take gift giving and reciprocity seriously as a foundational element of all social relations, we need to go behind the categories of modernization theory and the dichotomies it has implicated. One such dichotomy is the distinction between the formal and the informal, as noted above; another one is that separating the state from civil society (Alexander 1998; Putnam 2000). I do not deal extensively with the idea of civil society here, only allude to the seemingly enormous influence that ideas of an ideal form of civil society have had on social theory and our understanding of states. Basically the theory takes as its point of departure that there are fundamental differences between social relations within the boundaries and scope of the state, on the one hand, and life in associations, communities, and in part families (Bellah et al. 1985). It almost invariably leads to the conclusion that the two need to be separated, not least because the one is continuously in danger of invading the other (Habermas 1989). Yet the empirical record tells us that despite the assumption that they constitute entities and are driven by fundamentally different rationalities and social relations, there are in fact often few clearly delineated boundaries to be found. In Ulefoss, I found that the "bureaucratic" ethos constituting moral economy of membership was not at all a social order imposed by the state. Despite the fact that the municipal bureaucracy was an integral part of the postwar institutionalization of the Norwegian welfare state, municipal politics and administration were largely an extension of local, highly "modern," organizational forms.

The types of social relations found in any contemporary democratic society, if identified and distinguished through the lens of gift giving and reciprocity, do not seem to accord with the image of clear-cut boundaries implicated by categories such as "the state." One perspective from anthropology that offers itself for illustrating this is the analytical modeling of value circulation within and between "economic spheres." In Fredrik Barth's classic work on economic spheres in Darfur, Sudan, he showed how moral conventions regulated the production and circulation of value and prevented unwanted transgression (mixing value specific to one sphere with value circulating in another) from occurring (Barth 1996). Barth's study provides important insights into the logics of gift giving. Participating in a work party involves a specific morality defining what can be exchanged with what, and how. This legitimates certain social relationships and ties them to specific social contexts. When an Arab "entrepreneur" organizes a work party in order to plant tomato plants, he becomes able to seize value because tomato crops can be individually owned and tomatoes sold in the market for a price far exceeding the expenses involved in buying millet for the production of beer needed to attract participants to the work party.

The general message that can be drawn from this, as I see it, is that the moral economy of membership, as generally outlined above, involves in this perspective a conventional boundary between spheres of value.

The paramount moral boundary is the one that separates social status, superior knowledge (of the kind achieved though formal education, e.g.), and formal mandates (the right to lead or manage) from political influence, which (potentially or de facto) enables the collective of members to control political capital and the legitimate forms of gift giving. As I demonstrate later on in this book, this logic may not be limited to unions and political parties (the Labour Party in particular), but in fact expands and makes itself relevant in public institutions at the local level (the municipal institution in particular), thus preventing bureaucratic elites from utilizing the full potential of their formal mandates.

Although it is hardly original to state that forms of morally regulated reciprocity do not necessary follow formally established institutional boundaries, its implications have rarely been drawn except in instances where "traditional" social patterns seem to undermine the proper logic of "modern" institutions, or where local systems of production are incorporated in larger systems of capitalist exploitation. In light of my ethnographic material, which involves the social organization of politics in Norway (and to some extent Scandinavia at large), it seems that the contemporary ongoing centralization of the welfare state—mostly promoted as mechanisms that speed up and improve "modernization"—involves the reintroduction of forms of reciprocity that break radically with modernist ideas of democratic government. I hypothesize that they do so precisely by penetrating the spheres of exchange that, as in the case of Ulefoss, enabled horizontal political solidarity to become more or less immune to administrative cooptation through personal loyalty. The following example indicates that the forms of reciprocity that may prevent this type of penetration depend not only on the morality of membership in political parties, for example, the Labour Party in Ulefoss, but also on the possibility to extend it by means of horizontal alliances that cut across the boundaries of municipal/state institutions.

During my fieldwork in a Norwegian urban municipality in the mid-1990s (Vike 1996), in the town of Skien, just south of Ulefoss, I observed what to me appeared as a growing crisis in municipal welfare policy. Over a period of a few years, a number of local welfare offices had been closed down, and services and personnel were centralized to two units. Among the staff, there was a strong and shared experience that they suffered from lack of capacity, and they felt that they were unable to do their work properly. Unemployment was at a peak, and the largely industrial regional context encompassing the municipality was going through deep changes as it struggled to adjust to new economic realities. For welfare clients, this meant that they were now seen largely as the prototypical contrast to innovation and entrepreneurship, a symbol of bygone times and a burden to the municipal budget. The staff at the welfare office I studied felt that they lacked time and resources to work with the clients according to their own professional standards and their interpretation of state regulations, which aimed at assisting them, through more or less extensive counseling, in achieving more autonomy, and, ultimately, employment. Because of great labor market stress and economic decline, social workers felt their challenge was greater than ever before, as they experienced that the clients were worse off than ever and that the pressure from above to push them into the labor market in a situation of joblessness was quite unrealistic.

The Municipal Assembly had become highly critical of the office's increased spending, which had proven very hard to contain. I gradually realized that this situation was a result of a power struggle between the Assembly and the municipality's own welfare sector which had been escalating over several years. State regulations advised social workers to apply national regulations concerning welfare payments to clients, whereas the municipal authorities, due to tight budgets, demanded a lower standard. This was a deliberate choice on the part of the social workers; although their opposition to their employer was never made explicit, they clearly pursued a strategy of sabotage through informal coordination. This strategy included an alliance with several backbenchers in the Assembly, known to represent a critical opposition within the political parties. Several of the social workers were themselves active members of these parties. Thus, when local politicians from the speaker's position in the Assembly accused the staff at the welfare office of their lack of loyalty to their employer, most of those present were in fact in sympathy with the accused and contributed to preventing much political force from being invested in following up the accusations. This indicated to me that there were informal alliances at work that could be mobilized to protect the professional autonomy of the social workers.

State Building in Scandinavia: Some Key Characteristics

In Scandinavia, the gradual establishment of state apparatuses and state power followed a somewhat peculiar historical trajectory. Although similar to the British case in many ways, with a gradual and largely continuous, nonrevolutionary path towards democratization and univer-salization of citizen rights, the early modern state was much stronger and the (Danish and Swedish) aristocracy far less influential (Knudsen and Rothstein 1994). Moreover, the expansion of capitalism in Scandinavia, which was perhaps as forceful as in the British case, became more inclu-sive and not as systematically defined by large ownership, deep class divi-sions, and antagonisms based on wage labor on a massive scale (Stenius 2010). The most important difference, however, has probably to do with the role of popular involvement in the domains of the state, and its con-sequences. From early on the strong and highly centralized (and in part absolutist) Scandinavian states depended on cooperation by the farm-ing population, in part due to the power struggle with the aristocracy, and partly as a result of the desperate need for soldiers and taxes (Dyrvik 2011). In order to get access to these resources, rulers developed a form of governance that reasonably can be called *a direct form of indirect rule* (Vike 2017). The rulers of the states achieved direct access to the masses through local institutions that in part predated the state.

The result was, from a European perspective, an extraordinary mobi-lization of local interests in both the daily practical matters pertaining to health, religious rituals, schooling, agricultural innovation, property rights, and other judicial issues, but also more genuinely political mat-ters (Stenius 2010). It seems safe to say, furthermore, that the mobi-lization of political interest in Scandinavia assumed a particular and very homogeneous form: it manifested itself through the organization of collective interests through individual membership in highly egalitarian and strongly formalized associations (Sivesind and Selle 2010). Largely this organizational pattern reflected common local traditions for seeking solutions to labor scarcity (Lorentzen and Dugstad 2011). The capacity of the individual family to deal with labor scarcity related to agriculture, husbandry, fishing, and forestry, etc. was in most cases severely limited, as was its capacity to deal with the needy elderly, sick, the handicapped, and the poor. Women were heavily involved in all these activities, and their immediate interests related to their need to free themselves from overwhelming caring demands were an integrated aspect of what came to be seen as collective challenges for all households (Lin 2005). Associational life became practical tools for developing "public" solu-tions to such problems, and gradually associations also became more and more directly political. However, the political ethos that evolved in this context was not primarily one of rebellion and opposition, but one of building local infrastructure (services in the field of health, education, religion, finance, and transport, as well as conflict resolution, collective work, etc.) in ways that largely served the ambitions of state (access and control, increasing productivity, and more taxes) well (Stenius 2010; Dyrvik 2011).

One important aspect of this involvement was an increasing tendency to develop much broader agendas concerning societal improvement as well as national umbrella organizations. At the local level, such associations became both the environment and the social infrastructure of municipal politics and administration. Three additional features should be highlighted: associational life became by far the preferred form of social interaction, and contributed to generating an image of society and the state as a membership organization. Moreover, the membership base of associations became highly overlapping, members took part in many associations at once. Lastly, associations tended to develop normative universes characterized by strong, mutual social control, both through formal procedures, such as elections, and the use of extensive knowledge of individual persons and their commitment record (Selle 2013, 2016).

My own ethnographic experience of the dynamics of gift giving in associational life indicates that it tends to be quite strictly delineated both from private life and the hierarchical relations dominating institutions in the public sector and the market. The standard type of reciprocity seems to me the act of acknowledging fellow members as equals. The forms of exchange are "generalized" in Marshall Sahlins' sense (Sahlins 1965), but in a paradoxical way. They consist of a multitude of ways of offering recognition based on the will to make a voluntary effort to cultivate the common good and "take responsibility" by doing "more than one could reasonably expect," but the most striking aspect is perhaps the moral restrictions on what may be exchanged. Gentlemanly generosity, for example, and personal charity are generally sanctioned negatively and viewed as poisoned gifts. Behind the standard image of egalitarianism is a system of flexible hierarchical ranking based on individual effort and, in the case of those in elected positions, the ability to demonstrate a subordination to the will of the majority. In such a system most members are morally in debt, but very rarely in relation to other individuals, but to those who actually do most of the work on the behalf of others. "Moral debt" concerns those "creditors" who symbolically represent the association as a whole, and this debt is collectively handled though procedures and organizational rituals (celebrating enthusiasts ("souls of fire" in

Norwegian)). The prestige gained by members who make an extra effort may lead them into influential representative positions, but this also may create a moral generalized debt, in the sense that the mandate they are given has to be "repaid" in the form of symbolic respect for the collective interest. In this lies a potentially effective form of elite control, as well as the reciprocal basis for trust.

The inherent social tension in collectivities of this type consisted in the contradictory principles of commitment to the common good and, on the other hand, individual autonomy. The highly formalized nature of associational life in Scandinavia can be seen in light of this tension. Historically, membership became a means for the realization of structural and symbolic equality, and formal procedures a kind of guarantee that members kept a certain distance from each other. In my perspective, it is very difficult to explain the "collectivist" approach to dealing with political conflicts in Scandinavia without acknowledging the fundamentally "liberal" premise underlying it. Although the political struggle against "the state" in Norway (i.e., tax policies, but most importantly the behavior of local representatives of the King) was paramount in constituting forms of political contention from the fifteenth century onwards (see Chap. 4), in many cases the microsociological foundation for associational life was constituted by people's need for, and interest in, protecting themselves from the encroachment of others within the context of relationships that often involved extended forms of cooperation (Vike 2013).

The development of the first types of public services followed this logic. They enabled members to become less directly dependent on kin, neighbors, and the community at large. As members, they took part in the ownership and management of these services, which from early on were provided within a context of semi-professional organization. Thus, membership increasingly became a form of mediated reciprocity, or gift giving, if you will. Members cooperated in developing institutional arrangements that made them more autonomous in relation to each other. Interestingly, one of the hallmarks of the contemporary Scandinavian welfare state, the principle of universalism, seems inseparable from this kind of reciprocity. Although very often associated with a "generous" state, universalism originally served as an accentuation of membership egalitarianism in local communities. Although no doubt people were very unequal in several respects, the institutional logic of formalized associational life was one of acting as though they were equal. Inclusion and entitlement followed a very simple formula: if people could be helped to help themselves, everyone would benefit (Stenius 2010). This, in addition to the fact that needs testing is extremely costly and impractical favored a one-size-fits-all type of arrangement. Another important part of this was an emerging anticharity approach to service provision. Because acting as if people were equal constituted a basic premise for reciprocity, the pooling of resources (shared labor in particular), and commitment, the emerging system of service provision had to be crafted in way that secured this premise.

Thus, paradoxically, voluntary associations inspired an increasingly hostile attitude to volunteerism associated with charity, philanthropy, paternalism, and other forms of personal dependency resting on class difference (Seip 1994). Bureaucratically organized membership organizations became the dominant form of mobilizing political interest, constructing political alliances, solving practical (collective) problems, and securing egalitarian forms of social interaction, apparently for such reasons. The gift-giving dynamic between members was characterized by more or less shared commitments and many different forms and degrees of effort to construct and reproduce the common good, and contributed to securing a high degree of individual autonomy within the parameters of a conformist ethos (Stenius 2010). Members established a wide "transactional space" vis-à-vis each other, but salient values such as recognition, trust, and prestige circulated less between individual members directly than via the organization as a whole. People making an extra effort were seen as contributors to the organization as such, even in cases where their labor was invested in individual assistance to other members or some third party.

As Mike Savage and others have shown, this pattern is not "Scandinavian" in the sense of emerging from some specific, localized cultural tradition (Papakostas 2001; Savage 2005; Stenius 2010). But in Scandinavia, and in Norway in particular, it was to a great extent generalized and did not conflict sharply with state institutions. On the contrary, the organizational form and collective morality of voluntary organizations contributed quite heavily to form these institutions (Aronsson 1997). Decision-making procedures, leadership, the morality of public service, reciprocity, ideas of loyalty and solidarity, and even professional identities drew much of their inspiration from them. Hence, as the service-intense welfare state expanded from the 1960s onwards, and local municipalities became an institutional backbone of the state, local organizational, social, and moral forms amalgamated with state policy and control measures, thus establishing a very messy but at the same time highly efficient institutional form (Baldersheim et al. 1987; Baldersheim and Rose 2000). State-initiated welfare reforms, for example, were less extensions of managerial ambitions to increase control than a way to universalize experiments that had been carried out in municipalities. The great problem emerging from this institutional order and dynamic was the limitations to state control, and to the autonomy of state government. Indeed, in hindsight it may be reasonable to state that what Norwegian historian Francis Sejersted has called "The Social Democratic Era" (approximately from 1935 to 1980; Sejersted 2005), the public sector was not under anyone's control in the managerial sense of the word. The autonomy of municipalities and service-providing units and professions was extensive, and the potential success of policy changes initiated by the central state depended heavily on negotiation on a large scale. In the Nordic countries, about a third to two thirds of public employees work in municipalities, which spend an equivalent share of public resources (Baldersheim and Rose 2000: 17).

The "institutional ecology" of the Scandinavian welfare state historically emerged as a particular form of tension, cooperation, and, in part, amalgamation involving highly politically oriented voluntary associations, municipalities, and state power and bureaucratic rule. This made for a very homogeneous and unitary institutional system, but a very messy one at that. The emergence of the post-World War welfare state did not simply provide the basis for a strong central state, but reinforced the relative autonomy of municipalities, particularly through the exceptional growth of public service provision in this period. What I have called "the low level of gravity state" provided a relatively fertile ground for membership-based organizations (political parties primarily, but also other types of associations that work with and through them) and local social networks to influence politics. The distribution of power in any state society does not depend simply on the outcome of elections, but perhaps even more profoundly on how institutions may be subject to popular influence and control on a daily basis. This is a main theme in this book.

CHAPTER OUTLINE

In Chap. 2 I discuss some challenges involved in what anthropologists somewhat awkwardly have called "doing anthropology at home." I discuss this in relation to a review of some key characteristics of anthropology as a discipline, especially its development in the Norwegian context, and define my own position in relation to it. I also address some of the questions that seem to have fascinated observers of Scandinavia for a long time, especially as these questions concern trust in institutions and in "the state."

The third chapter presents a case study of local welfare policy in Norway, from the Skien municipality. It provides an in-depth exploration of how local politicians develop arguments as they try to deal with dilemmas in decision making, and describes how they reach consensus. However, the process takes a new turn when they, after having chosen a rebellious stand towards "elite politicians in all parties," realize they face an administration that rejects adhering to their path of action and instead chooses loyalty to their superiors. The local politicians' mobilization of horizontal alliances across the boundaries of the municipal organization thus fails, and in this chapter I discuss what this means. The managerial order that is established during the process may, for example, be seen as a "historical moment" involving an invasion into the morality of membership and primacy of political representation of a particular kind.

In Chap. 4 I take a step back and look more closely at the politics of solidarity, inspired by Peter Baldwin's classic discussion of how, in democratic states, horizontal social relations become politicized and may serve as vehicles of class alliances and political influence. The emergence of the welfare state needs to be explained, as does the principle of universalism, one of the hallmarks of the Scandinavian Model. In this chapter, I argue that the welfare state and the principle of universalism are tightly interwoven. I demonstrate how Anthony Giddens' vision of "The New Egalitarianism" and what Lewis Minkin has called "The Blair Supremacy" represent a reintroduction of elitism and personal dependency, and suggest that this constitutes a more serious threat than the largely misplaced and often deeply romantic scholarly criticism of bureaucracy. The Norwegian version of the welfare state is here seen in the light of more general changes in state form.

Chapter 5 offers a historical perspective on the emergence of political resistance, and its constitutive role in state formation in Norway and

Scandinavia. It provides a review of some important instances of political challenges to state power from below. In addition, it includes an attempt to sketch some important phases in state building and state institutions in Denmark/Norway leading up to the present. I try to substantiate my claim that municipal politics in Norway have generally been heavily influenced by organized interests (trust networks) which to some extent have been able to challenge the logics of state governance, and assume that the relative success of such challenges may in part explain the emergence of the welfare state as we know it. In Norway in particular, local institutions—municipalities, above all—have been key arenas for the social organization of political interests, and have only partially served as extensions of state power.

In Chap. 6 I return to the municipality of Skien and discuss, through a case study of a municipal reorganizational process, how managerial interests struggle to achieve control over the organization. Also, it is shown that municipal employees have alternative pathways of action, and do not necessarily comply with the ideology of loyalty and managerial control. Moreover, the chapter shows how the consequences of control measures affect different categories of municipal employees, and how these employees perceive their role in the organization and the wider context of the welfare state, more or less "betwixt and between" their role as advocates of universalism and the users/local population, on the one hand, and municipal functionaries.

The following chapter (Chap. 7) describes the relationship between the central state, the municipality, and the street-level bureaucrats. The case in point is elder care, which serves as an illustration of the welfare state's capacity problem. As the overwhelming majority of the street-level bureaucrats in municipal service provision are women, the capacity problem seems to be dealt with through a highly gendered synthesis of policymaking and organizational governance. I demonstrate how the central state and the municipalities utilize this resource, how its uses are negotiated, and how the gradual appropriation of municipal and professional autonomy by the central state influences service quality and, in the long run, seems to undermine universalism. In this chapter, the analytical distinction between what I call utopian time and contemporary time is used in order to illuminate how a certain temporal asymmetry serves as a mechanism for decentralizing responsibility and dilemma, while centralizing power.

In Chap. 8, I move on to describe a very different world, that of psychotherapy. Here I explore ways in which psychotherapy draws on the wider cultural context in which it is embedded, and choose in particular to look at the idea of individual autonomy. When trying to find ways to understand and develop mental health promoting patterns of social interaction, therapists and patients draw on a repertoire of meanings embedded in cultural history. In the Norwegian context, individual autonomy and egalitarianism constitute important parts of this repertoire (Sørensen and Stråth 1997). In the first part of the chapter, I focus on family therapy, which, to me, serves as a particularly interesting illumination of these themes. The second part elaborates another major and related theme in this book: how specific institutional contexts play an important role in assisting people in constructing worldviews, organizational boundaries in particular.

The concluding chapter (Chap. 9) sums up my perspective on the emergence of the contemporary welfare state, and offers some reflections on what it means to explore "the state" by moving in and out of institutions, focusing on social relations rather than on models of how institutions are supposed to work. I argue that egalitarian politics have much to do with the control of institutions from "below" through mechanisms of social control that are embedded in the morality of membership. The reintroduction of forms of governance and institutional control based on personal loyalty and other "traditional" relational properties, I point out, represents a fundamental challenge for the welfare state. Its potential for becoming an authoritarian state form, as opposed to a common good and a relatively open institutional system allowing for change and correction through participation, resistance, and sabotage, seems strongly reinforced by such changes, as does its capacity for undermining the main mechanisms that made the welfare state possible in the first place, such as the principle of universalism.

REFERENCES

Alexander, Jeffrey. (ed.). 1998. *Real Civil Societies. Dilemmas of Institutionalization.* London: Sage Press.

Aronsson, Petter. 1997. Local Politics–The Invisible Political Culture. In *The Cultural Construction of Norden*, ed. Øystein Sørensen and Bo Stråth, 172–206. Oslo: Scandinavian University Press.

Baldersheim, Harald et al. 1987. *Folkestyre i by og bygd. Norske kommuner gjennom 150 år.* Oslo: Universitetsforlaget.

Baldersheim, Harald, and Lawrence E. Rose. 2000. *Det kommunale laboratorium. Teoretiske perspektiver på kommunal organisering.* Bergen: Fagbokforlaget.

Barth, Fredrik. 1996. *Manifestasjon og prosess.* Oslo: Universitetsforlaget.

Bellah, Robert N., et al. 1985. *Habits of the Heart. Commitment and Individualism in American Life.* Berkeley: University of California Press.

Brøgger, Jan. 1990. *Pre-Bureaucratic Europeans. A Study of a Portuguese Fishing Community.* Oslo: Norwegian University Press.

Collins, Randall. 2011. Patrimonial Alliances and Failures of State Penetration: A Historical Dynamic of Crime. Corruption, Gangs, and Mafias. *The Annals of the American Academy of Political and Social Sciences* 636, June: 16–31.

Douglas, Mary. 1986. *How Institutions Think.* New York: Syracuse University Press.

Dyrvik, Ståle. 2011. *Norsk historie 1536–1814: Vegar til sjølvstende.* Oslo: Samlaget.

Fassin, Didier, et al. 2013. *At the Heart of the State. He Moral Worlds of Institutions.* London: Pluto Press.

Friedmann, John. 1987. *Planning in the Public Domain. From Knowledge to Action.* Princeton: Princeton University Press.

Graubard, Stephen R. (ed.). 1986. *Norden: The Passion for Equality.* Oslo: Norwegian University Press.

Habermas, Jürgen. 1989. *The Structural Transformation of the Public Sphere: An Inquiry into a Category of Bourgeois Society.* Cambridge: MIT Press.

Herzfeld, Michael. 1992. *The Social Production of Indifference. Exploring the Symbolic Roots of Western Bureaucracy.* Chicago: The University of Chicago Press.

Iversen, Torben, and Soskice David. 2006. Electoral Institutions and the Politics of Coalitions: Why Some Democracies Redistribute More than Others. *American Political Science Review* 100 (2): 165–181.

Kildal, Nanna, and Kuhnle Stein. 2005. The Nordic Welfare Model and the Idea of Universalism. In *Normative Foundations of the Welfare State. The Nordic Experience,* ed. Nanna Kildal and Stein Kuhnle. New York: Routledge.

Knudsen, Tim, and Bo Rothstein. 1994. State Building in Scandinavia. *Comparative Politics* 26 (2): 203–220.

Kronenfeld, David B. 2008. *Culture, Society, and Cognition. Collective Goals, Values, Action, and Knowledge.* Berlin: Mouton de Gruyter.

Lin, Ka. 2005. Cultural Traditions and the Scandinavian Social Policy Model. *Social Policy & Administration* 39 (7): 723–739.

Lorentzen, Håkon, and Line Dugstad. 2011. *Den norske dugnaden.* Kristiansand: Høyskoleforlaget.

Papakostas, Apostolis. 2001. Why is There No Clientelism in Sweden? In *Clientelism, Interests, and Democratic Representation. The European Experience in Historical and Comparative Perspective*, ed. Simona Piattoni, 31–54. Cambridge: Cambridge University Press.

Parsons, Talcott. 1964. *Essays in Sociological Theory*. New York: Free Press.

Piattoni, Simona (ed.). 2001. *Clientelism, Interests, and Democratic Representation. The European Experience in Historical and Comparative Perspective*. Cambridge: Cambridge University Press.

Putnam, Robert D. 2000. *Bowling Alone. The Collapse and Revival of American Community*. New York: Simon & Schuster.

Roniger, Luis. 1998. Civil Society, Patronage, and Democracy. In *Real Civil Societies. Dilemmas of Institutionalization*, ed. Jeffrey Alexander, 66–84. London: Sage.

Sahlins, Marshall. 1965. On the Sociology of Primitive Exchange. In *The Relevance of Models in Social Anthropology*, ed. Michael Banton, 139–186. London: Tavistock.

Savage, Mike. 2005. The Popularity of Bureaucracy: Involvement in Voluntary Associations. In *The Values of Bureaucracy*, ed. Paul Du Gay, 309–335. Oxford: Oxford University Press.

Seip, Anne Lise. 1994. *Sosialhjelpstaten blir til. Norsk sosialpolitikk 1740–1920*. Oslo: Gyldendal.

Sejersted, Francis. 2005. *Sosialdemokratiets tidsalder: Norge og Sverige i det 20. århundre*. Oslo: Pax.

Selle, Per. 2013. Reflektioner kring medlemsmodellens betydelse. In *Civilsamhället klämt mellan stat och kapital: välfärd, mångfald, framtid*, ed. Lars Trägårdh et al., 49–63. Stockholm: SNS Forlag.

Selle, Per. 2016. Frivillighetens marginalisering. *Tidsskrift for velferdsforskning* 19 (1): 76–89.

Sivesind, Karl Henrik, and Per Selle. 2010. Civil Society in the Nordic Countries: Between Displacement and Vitality. In *Nordic Associations in a European Perspective*, eds. Stenius, Henrik, and Risto, Alapuro. Baden-Baden: Nomos.

Sørensen, Øystein, and Bo Stråth. 1997. *The Cultural Construction of Norden*. Oslo: Scandinavian University Press.

Stenius, Henrik. 2010. Nordic Associational Life in a European and an Inter-Nordic Perspective. In *Nordic Associations in a European Perspective*, ed. Henrik Stenius and Risto Alapuro. Nomos: Baden-Baden.

Thelen, Tatjana, Larissa Vetters, and Keebet von Benda-Beckmann. 2014. Introduction to Stategraphy. Toward a Relational Anthropology of the State. *Social Analysis* 58 (3): 1–19.

Vike, Halvard. 1991. *Contested Signs: Political Discourse in a Norwegian Industrial Community*. Thesis, University of Oslo: Department of Social Anthropology.

Vike, Halvard. 1996. *Conquering the Unreal: Politics and Bureaucracy in a Norwegian Town*. Thesis, University of Oslo: Department of Social Anthropology.

Vike, Halvard. 1997. Reform and Resistance. A Norwegian Illustration. In *Anthropology of Policy: Critical Perspectives on Governance and Power*, ed. Chris Shore and Susan Wright, 150–165. London: Routledge.

Vike, Halvard. 2012. Varianter av vest-europeiske statsformasjoner—Utkast til en historisk antropologi. *Norsk antropologisk tidsskrift* 23 (2): 126–142.

Vike, Halvard. 2013. Egalitarianisme og byråkratisk individualisme. *Norsk antropologisk tidsskrift* 24 (3–4): 181–193.

Vike, Halvard and Haukelien Heidi. 2017. Family Therapy and Holistic Complexity–An Ethnographic Approach to Therapeutic Practice in a Norwegian Psychiatric Clinic. In *Routine Outcome Monitoring in Couple and Family Therapy. The Empirically Informed Therapist*, ed. Terje Tilden and Bruce Wampold, 173–189. Cham: Springer.

Wolf, Eric. 1966. Kinship, Friendship, and Patron-Client Relations in Complex Societies. In *The Social Anthropology of Complex Societies*, ed. Michael Banton, 1–23. London: Tavistock Publications.

CHAPTER 2

No Direction Home?
Doing Anthropology in Norway

ON "HOME BLINDNESS"

When watching Martin Scorsese's documentary about Bob Dylan, *No Direction Home*, one inevitably gets the impression that Dylan wants to tell us that he actually came from nowhere. Hibbing, Minnesota, where Dylan grew up, is referred to only as a bleak general place in the shadow of Dylan's fame, and according to commentator Roger Ebert (2005) he "mentions his father only because he bought the house where Dylan found a guitar." It is very hard to grasp where the point of view from which Dylan sees the world comes from, and what influenced him prior to his arrival in New York City. I want to suggest that anthropologists, perhaps somewhat like Dylan, often tend to appear as people from nowhere studying others as locals, those who are socially embedded in worlds more or less radically different from that of the anthropologist. It is illustrative, therefore, that anthropologists tend to talk about doing anthropology in the country where they are born and socialized as "doing anthropology at home" (Jackson 1987; Gullestad 2011). Perhaps because they perceive of themselves as possessing an abstraction of identity, they tend to see any local spot in the country in which they grew up as a version of their "home," or "their own" place. In my understanding, this positioning is not well suited for understanding what she or he really shares with those studied or learns by studying them, nor what it is that may be different. The position disposes anthropologists to claim familiarity on false premises. Claiming familiarity in this way echoes

© The Author(s) 2018
H. Vike, *Politics and Bureaucracy in the Norwegian Welfare State,*
Approaches to Social Inequality and Difference,
https://doi.org/10.1007/978-3-319-64137-9_2

Ernest Gellner's portrait of the European enlightened elites in the era of revolutionary nationalism: these elites insisted that every peasant was a natural emblem of the nation, and gave the peasants a slot in the greater narrative of the elite's burden to represent the whole and classify them (Gellner 1983).

Surely, the metaphor of "doing anthropology at home" is a bad one. That is why, I argue, anthropologists' discussions of the special pitfalls they may sink into and the challenges this represents for the discipline tend to miss the point. How is it possible that people so well trained in contextualizing other people actually consider a whole territory called a country or a nation their "home"?

If we try to move beyond the metaphor of "home" and look more closely at the anthropological discourse of problematic familiarity, that is, familiarity of the kind that supposedly makes anthropologists "home blind," clearly the main problem is epistemological rather than a property of the object of study. Very few anthropologists have reported that they, as "natives," automatically blended so well with their informants that they failed to deal with them anthropologically. On the other hand, the claim that it is unattractive, uninteresting, and/or not fascinating enough to do fieldwork "at home" is indeed quite commonly made, at least in anthropological seminars. The debate about the construction of otherness in anthropology is clearly linked to a certain distaste for what we construct as familiar, ordinary, and perhaps socially awkward on a more personal plane. Ideas of what "home" is, where it is located, is reflected in specific anthropological constructions of culture, that is, culture as somehow linked to a nation; as difference of the kind that produces culture shock and/or visible boundaries; or as an aspect of clearly delineated and homogeneous social groups, "little traditions," and communities. This may in part explain why anthropologists have largely left the study of the major institutions of Western society to sociologists, economists, and political scientists. Also, it brings to light what appears as what Frederic Jameson has called a "strategy of containment": fieldwork in contexts that mobilize the familiarity syndrome in the anthropologist brings her into situations where informants tend to make claims directly related to the anthropologist's social status and taste, and most probably her political interests, too (Jørgensen 2017).

Marilyn Strathern, in her discussion of "auto-anthropology" in Anthony Jackson's edited book, *Anthropology at Home* (1987), insists, if I have understood her correctly, that the salient feature of doing anthropology "at home" is that anthropologists and those under study are somehow in the same business of creating accounts of culture and society. Her concern is not so much the social relationship between these actors and the way it influences anthropological epistemology, but one of overlapping genres. Anthropological accounts are "continuous with indigenous form," and the anthropological endeavor is no longer one of translating one culture into the terms of another. Clearly, this perspective is fruitful and helps us reformulate problems of familiarity, but as far as I can understand, there is a problem. Strictly speaking the continuity is not between anthropological accounts of "indigenous form" as such, because "indigenous form" is a concept we use to describe a certain general pattern, a pattern generated by differentiated social realities consisting of many different and often conflicting voices and interests, as well as shifting contexts. In the following, partly inspired by Strathern's discussion, I look more closely at how this specific form of continuity has developed in anthropological studies of Norwegian society, arguing that there may be no such thing as a supposedly unitary indigenous form.

ASPECTS OF THE ETHNOGRAPHY OF NORWAY

In Norway, anthropology "at home" started in the classical manner as a study of the primitives within. The great ancestor in Norwegian sociology, Eilert Sundt (1817–1875), conducted fieldwork among the lower classes around the mid-1800s. His work began as a search for why civilization failed to take root among the lower classes, but later it became a source for serious reflection on the relationship between social inequality and ways of life (see Sundt 2006). For a number of reasons, including perhaps the tradition Sundt initiated, modern social anthropology in Norway never developed a clear hegemonic idea of the prototypical object of study, and thus it created a space for students with very different motivations. In fact, doing fieldwork in Norway became accepted and commonplace and Norwegian ethnography came to be seen as a natural part of the total repertoire. When I entered the master's program in social anthropology in Oslo in 1990, I got the impression that two things were paramount: doing good fieldwork, which meant mapping social interaction ethnographically, and analyzing data in terms of a processual and comparative perspective. The discipline was expanding rapidly, and student numbers exploded. There was little discussion about the boundaries of the discipline; rather, there was a strong sense of identity and even a certain eagerness to explore the territories of neighboring disciplines. To the public, anthropology came to be seen not as the study of the Other per se, or of the little society, but as a different and largely refreshing, comparative perspective on politically relevant issues. Nevertheless, a certain scepticism towards carrying out fieldwork in Norway was cultivated among a few Norwegian anthropologists. Part of the reason was that some of my teachers tended to think this represented an epistemological challenge of a particular kind. The argument was that it is hard to learn anything genuinely new when there is no real culture shock involved.

Nevertheless, the anthropological study of Norway includes a relatively extensive fascination with the nonexotic and the mainstream. A main contributor to this effect is Marianne Gullestad. In the context of this book, her identification of "sameness" as a powerful mechanism of making equality real in social interaction is particularly significant. In Norway, she argues, it is very common to insist that meaningful interaction can only take place as long as those involved de-emphasize differences between them, particularly differences pertaining to rank (Gullestad 1989: 109–123). Gullestad's first major work was a study of an old working-class neighborhood in Norway's second largest town, Bergen (Gullestad 1984). In this and later works on related themes, she found that class was only peripherally relevant to how people with different class backgrounds identified themselves. Working-class people tended to see themselves as having the same set of values as anyone else except snobbish people and deviant individuals. The insight echoes Jan Petter Blom's classic study of mountain farmers and valley farmers of inland South Norway, published in *Ethnic Groups and Boundaries* (1969). Although mountain farmers saw themselves as different from their more affluent valley neighbors, they largely embraced the values of these significant others and tried, if ambivalently, to adopt these values. Blom demonstrated that his case was one of inverted ethnicity. Although mountain farmers fulfilled all the basic criteria of an ethnic group vis-à-vis their valley neighbors, as anthropologists had identified these in the study of symbiotic relations between the various groups of SouthEast Asia in particular, they still, at the same time, embraced the "modern," bourgeoisie, or middle-class oriented values of the valley farmers in part because to them these values represented a vehicle for social mobility. Gullestad's and Blom's observations would indicate that in Norway, there may be rather strong cultural currents working against cultural segmentation, despite the fact that cultural differences which could turn into ethnicities and categorical boundaries based on social class can be found all over the place. How are we to understand this in broader analytical terms?

In several later works by Norwegian anthropologists looking at aspects of Norwegian culture, a key assumption is that the peasant heritage is still strong, and that the normal life of a modern class-based, capitalist society—influenced primarily by life in the metropolis—has somehow not yet found its way into the patterns of national culture. In *Totemism, the Norwegian Way—Reflections on the Nature of the Norwegian Social Democracy*, Tian Sørhaug touches on the problem of morality (Sørhaug 1986). Public morality in Norwegian society, he argues, is a product of the metaphorical power of the close-knit community where everyone knows everyone else. This inclines the population to see the national polity as consisting of people essentially of the same kind. The other side of the coin is that Norwegians, so immersed in this not yet fully modernized cultural system, have a hard time developing a critical distrustful attitude to their leaders and the institutions they run, as long as they seem to follow the rules and look OK. In small communities, everyone tends to think that all have identical interests, he adds. In several publications, Marianne Gullestad argues in a somewhat similar vein, emphasizing that "egalitarian individualism" has a lot to do with Norwegians' love for their home (see Gullestad 2002). Two closely related observations made by Gullestad are worth mentioning: that the home serves as an important metaphorical inspiration for the idea of a nation of equals, and that people's love for their home somehow makes them able to resist the pressure from markets and bureaucracies dominating the public domain (Gullestad 1989: 175).

> In contemporary folk theory, the home, the family and the intimate sphere represent a sharp contrast to big society, particularly bureaucratic organization. The intimate sphere constitutes a space where people feel a sense of control, and where bureaucracy, according to most people, should not be allowed to expand. In a very special way the home represents intimacy, privacy, wholeness and the personal, in contrast to the bureaucratic, instrumental, efficient, and specialized. (Gullestad 1989: 175. My translation)

In order to establish a critical angle on the assumptions put forth by Sørhaug and Gullestad we may turn to John Barnes' work in Western Norway in the 1950s (Barnes 1954). He demonstrated that the egalitarian ethos and the organization of trust in close-knit informal networks were intimately related to community politics (as opposed to the home and "traditional" arenas). Barnes (1954) identified "committees and class" as salient features of the local world he observed. According to Barnes, Bremnes and other peripheral areas of Norway were characterized by the void of a conventional state apparatus due to the Norwegian separation from Denmark (in 1814, and later from Sweden in 1905); the local politics he observed were gradually filling this political void. The committees represented "a common pattern of organization which occurs in every instance of formal social life" (p. 50), that is, a committee for each association, elected by an annual meeting, and an executive council, a chairman, treasurer, and a secretary: all based on the simple majority vote. Barnes further speculated what type of social class system Bremnes would turn out to be in the future. He saw the social process he described—a "gradual emergence of part-time peasants in key positions of government"—as necessarily transitional. He expected increasing class differences to undermine both the role of part-time peasants and that of the committees. In Bremnes, at the time of Barnes' fieldwork, social inequality was clearly present, but the strongly egalitarian code of behavior seemed to make it largely irrelevant. Barnes assumed that this situation would change as inequality grew stronger. He observed that Bremnes "part-time peasants" involved themselves in commercial trading with fish from very early on; in much the same way as "peasants" in other parts of the country did, mainly in the timber trade. At the time of his fieldwork, the fishing industry was expanding, establishing what Barnes saw as a more "modern" system of hierarchical relations than the ones he observed in politics and social networks in the community. Although Barnes' perspective clearly differs from that of Gullestad and Sørhaug in that he acknowledges the significance of "public culture" and the power of politics in forming identities and social organization, he seemed to share their assumption that the reality he observed was somehow not fully modernized. In other words, they were "traditional" and on the margins of something else, more modern.

Nevertheless, Barnes' pioneering interest in political activity among "part-time peasants" demonstrated that his informants were members of formally organized committees that overlapped with informal networks of kin, neighbors, friends, and workmates. In Bremnes, the idea of egalitarianism emerged as a combination of a worldview, certain universal citizen rights, a style of interaction, and, perhaps above all, an institutional mechanism for dealing with political conflict. Barnes emphasized that political conflict, when channeled through discussions in the committees and the Municipal Assembly, mostly ended up in unanimous votes. Although in his account the description of how this was actually done, who the actors where, who they represented, what their aims were, how they thought about what they were doing, and so on, is quite thin, it is also fascinating. First of all, Barnes indicates that the formal roles and relationships assumed by local actors in political activity were of primary importance. These roles and relationships did not constitute a layer on top of other identities related to kinship, neighborhood, and the like, but, at least to a large extent, substituted them. Second, the matters they dealt with in these formal capacities were not private or quasi-private, but genuinely public ones. Finally, it seems that these roles and relationships contributed strongly to shape the local people's social ontology, that is, their idea of what kinds of people lived in the Bremnes community. As they saw it, Bremnes people were overwhelmingly common folks. They knew that in the wider region, there were some "fine people," but they were found almost exclusively in Bergen, the regional center. In addition, there existed a few families and individuals with special problems and who needed some public (municipal) assistance. Local folks all seemed to be aware of the fact that people were not equal, literally speaking, but in politics and associational life at large, they treated each other as though they were: one man, one vote.

As is the case in the other Nordic countries and Germany, modern anthropology in Norway relates to ethnology and folklore studies, leaving the discipline with some potentially problematic ties. However, Fredrik Barth's great influence from the early 1950s onwards gave anthropology a much more distinct identity as a social science of the new kind. Clearly, in order to reinforce that identity, Barth defined anthropology as something that stood in opposition to neighboring disciplines, the human sciences in particular. Anthropology became a fieldwork-based, comparative, and cross-cultural study of social process in a synchronic perspective as opposed to a study of the cultural past of "a people." This had some great advantages, some of which Barth himself may have never intended. As a social science proper, anthropology was able to tap into the great prestige and influence that sociology and political science had already acquired with the Norwegian public, partly as a result of the great breakthrough of economic science in political planning in the 1930s onwards. In Norway in the fifties and sixties, social science was institutionalized in highly autonomous academic institutions, and most social scientists seemed to share a strong motivation to use their autonomy to influence government policy and involve themselves in public debate. The first anthropological manifestation of this tendency was Fredrik Barth's initiative to take a closer look at entrepreneurship in northern Norway, which brought anthropologists in close contact with the large-scale state governmental attempt to engineer social change. In his introduction to the anthology, *The Role of the Entrepreneur in Social Change in Norway* (1962), Barth stated that "[V]ery frequently entrepreneurship involves the relationship between persons and institutions of one society with those of another, economically more advanced one, and the entrepreneur becomes an essential 'broker' in this situation of culture contact" (Barth 1962: 5).

Shortly after, one of Barth's students and a contributor to the anthology, Ottar Brox, wrote the book, *What's Happening in Northern Norway?* (1966), that was aimed at the general public and had a very clear political message. Brox was inspired by dependency theory and brought it to bear directly on the issue of "culture contact." Arguing that the traditional adaptation along the coast of northern Norway, that of fishermen/farmers, or "part-time peasants," as Barnes called them, was highly rational and efficient, and both economically and ecologically highly viable, Brox demonstrated that the government's plan to modernize the region by means of massive industrialization would have far-reaching, unintended consequences. Brox hit a nerve in Norwegian society. The book became a key reference for the growing antiurban, antiauthoritarian, environmentalist-leftist movement in the 1960s and 1970s, which culminated in the first "No to the EU" vote in 1972. The electoral landslide that followed immediately after brought Brox himself a seat in the Parliament. Through this book, and many other later works, Brox demonstrated anthropology's relevance for understanding contemporary politics in a novel way. He showed how ethnography could strengthen our understanding of political institutions, how institutions generate worldviews (or political ideology), and how the analysis of people's lives in contemporary Norwegian society could be understood in the context of political economy. In my own work, including the present book, Brox is a major inspiration.

As were most other students attracted by Barth's intellectual depth and charisma, Ottar Brox cared little for cultural history. The emphasis was on the here and now. The confidence in the synchronic perspective was so great that anthropologists could use it to write the history of the future, as in Brox's case, and reconstruct the past in terms of the present, as Barth had tried to do in his work on Swat Pathans (Barth 1959). Perhaps more important, Ottar Brox did not seem to care much about the fact that northern Norway was "home" to him. Although his work in part was inspired by Barth's idea of the entrepreneurial domain as an interface between cultures, he, like his teacher, was mostly concerned with political economy, institutions and microcontexts, not cultures.

In fact, the same can be said of many other Norwegian anthropologists of Brox's generation, especially those who included a feminist inspiration in their approach (Rudie 1984; Holtedahl 1986). The study of households as a prism for social change caught the attention of many, and had far-reaching implications for the anthropology of Norway and beyond. What these anthropologists did, among other things, was to develop models for understanding the institutionalization of the social democratic state at the local level. A key figure here was Marianne Gullestad (1984, 1989, 1992, 2001, 2002, 2011). As indicated above, through a long series of contributions Gullestad took the household orientation many steps further and opened several new analytical paths that have ever since been extremely influential among colleagues and students. Gullestad's originality lies in part in her ability to analyze these phenomena as a part of the everyday life of members of the majority culture, without ever making culture into some bounded whole. Her theory of the Nordic version of "egalitarian individualism" is a relevant case in point. According to Gullestad, "egalitarian individualism" is to be seen as an interactional style, or code of behavior, and is about the pragmatic agreement between social actors that in order to relate meaningfully to each other, the relations must rest on the mutual acknowledgment of "sameness."

It should be pointed out here that unlike Barth, Brox, and their followers, Barnes did in fact care about history. In an attempt to contextualize his analysis of Bremnes as a highly egalitarian community, he noted that Norway didn't really have a state until quite recently. The end of Danish colonial rule created a vacuum in rural areas which brought "part-time peasants into key positions in the structure of government and organized social life." Barnes' underlying assumption that, as a result of the postcolonial vacuum, modernization had taken place at a relatively late stage, has, as shown above, surfaced in many later anthropological versions of Norway. Surely it has stimulated the idea that after all there is something exotic to be found here. Yet Barnes' most important contribution (in addition to inventing network as an analytical concept) has never seemed to have been systematically followed up in anthropological studies of Scandinavia: his fascinating ethnographic mapping of how patterns of interaction and power were intimately linked with the way in which people moved in and out of institutions. Gullestad became mainly concerned with everyday life in private and informal contexts, and later with public discourse, and Barth's and Brox's early interest in such matters was seemingly never linked to Barnes nor followed up by others in any systematic manner.

As far as I can see, the most important question in Barnes' study with a direct relevance to cultural history is what it meant for people in Bremnes to be members of what he called "committees." In order to understand this, it is important to bear in mind that the committees he studied constituted the backbone of institutionalized municipal politics. At the same time they were part of a wider system of overlapping memberships in a variety of formally organized institutions that served collective interests. In comparative terms this is significant mainly because the political and economic interests that gave rise to such institutions, voluntary organizations, as they are called in the civil society genre, were of fundamental interest to most people in Bremnes and were definitely not simply created in a power vacuum nor introduced by the modernizing Norwegian state. In fact, the coastal regions of Norway, as well as inland areas from which timber could be transported along waterways, were among the most expansive preindustrial economies in Europe. Even more important, there were few possibilities for monopolizing fish, timber, and the channels of value they opened (Dyrvik 1979). And because the labor necessary to extract these sources of value was scarce, labor was organized in much the same way as were traditional work parties among peasants and organized resistance against representatives of the Danish state. It is not a wild generalization to state that in economic and political terms, Scandinavia was "modernized" very early and in somewhat different terms than in many other areas of Europe (Ibid.). Capitalist expansion was indeed thorough, but it took a much more local form than in most of the rest of Europe, and was much less monopolist. And because the old elites were never really capable of crushing or pacifying popular movements as these became politicized, only curbing them, these movements may represent a deeper continuity in Scandinavia than in most other parts of Europe, where the state has been much more successful in reproducing preindustrial forms of authority and hierarchy.

As indicated in Chap. 1, being a member of a voluntary organization seems to be strongly associated with a specific form of morality.
Finnish historian Henrik Stenius has grasped this phenomenon well in
his chapter, "The Good Life Is a Life in Conformity," in Sørensen and
Stråth's important edited volume, *The Cultural Construction of Norden*
(1997). In his terms, a key emergent property of voluntary associations
that manage collective interests is conformity. According to Stenius, this
particular way of managing collective goods (i.e., through the horizontal
solidarity of membership rather than hierarchical command and personal
dependency) stimulates informal control of a kind that often tends to be
reinforced by formal membership. This is Gullestad's egalitarian individualism revisited, but with a different source than informal everyday life.
In voluntary organizations of this type, politics is everywhere at all times.
Mutual social control often seems to include most aspects of life because
the management of the common good depends on trust, and trust in
turn tends to rest on rich information concerning people's behavior. This
may be why the preference for formally organizing social relations of all
kinds has been so strong in the Nordic region; it allows for control over
collectively controlled resources, and provides people with the possibility to keep a distance from each other, a formula that in part sums up a
Nordic version of individual autonomy. Stenius' main point, however, is
that in the Nordic countries this morality was generalized, heavily influencing not only social relations in local communities but also the public
sphere and to some extent even the state.

A very good illustration here is the temperance movement in the early
nineteenth century (Stenius 2010). The temperance movement grew out
of local concerns, but very soon, it gained significant national influence.
Simply speaking, its goal was to make the way from work to home as
short as possible for working-class men, thereby inspiring a certain distaste for places where they could congregate without some useful common purpose. Its agenda, a very restrictive, and partly aggressive (or
perhaps we should say generous) preventive alcohol policy, was translated to national policy quickly and without much hesitation. It is quite
remarkable that it has not, as of yet, stimulated a general opposition
against the state's right to invade civil society and private lives.

BALANCING INSTITUTIONAL POWER

In my own research on local politics and bureaucracy, I have been inspired by the possibility of following people as they move in and out of institutions. By studying local politics in Norway ethnographically, I have attempted to explore the ways in which public institutions are socially embedded, and how people use them to make claims and attempt to keep them under some control. Public services are largely provided by municipalities, and because there is little doubt that people's confidence in the state in this region of Europe is largely about access to attractive public services, the social organization of municipal politics is of great anthropological interest. However, a general analytical problem is that studies of the state tend to be split into two unfruitful extremes. In political science, it is largely influenced by images and models drawn from the state itself. In anthropology, a general ignorance seems to exist concerning the study of the institutional apparatus of the state based on ethnographic data. For this reason, it may be relevant to turn our attention to classical studies of "stateless" societies. These studies were often guided by an ambition to grasp institutional dynamics on a large scale, and to explain the reproduction of power without reference to the visible hand of a sovereign agent with a unitary form and function. Naturally, they did not take the versions provided by powerful agents at face value, but needed to focus on what they did and the patterns implicated by their actions. Fredrik Barth, in his analysis of leadership among Swat Pathans (1959), looked at the phenomenon of crosscutting ties and its implications for political power and conflict, the same problem that concerned Max Gluckman in *The Peace in the Feud* (1955). Their message, simply put, was that crosscutting ties may turn political conflict into institutional order at a higher level. Shifting alliances may prevent the monopolization of power and balance it in the long run. Power is shared, but no one is in a position to control the dynamics of sharing.

In my research on local politics in Norway, I have observed that overlapping membership gives rise to what we may call a culture of negotiation, one that often effectively penetrates and challenges the boundaries between bureaucracy, politics, and civil society. Well-organized resistance against municipal policies may indeed succeed, and because the alliances that make such moves possible tend to be context specific, they rarely give rise to fundamental cleavages. The pattern emerging from this dynamic seems to have two key elements: the application of bureaucratic rules easily becomes politicized and requires negotiations, depending on the degree and nature of political mobilization; and political leaders have to be very careful about stretching their mandate, and administrative leaders often need to check out what their employees think, as the latter sometimes ally themselves with politicians and voluntary organizations that have a stake in a given policy. Formal and informal types of control operate simultaneously, and to some extent prevent the municipal hierarchy from becoming pyramidal and powerful actors from demanding personal loyalty from others. Consequently, when using their rights as members as leverage, actors both within and outside the institution have the power to make claims that go beyond formal specifications of rights and duties. At the same time, perhaps precisely for that reason, they all tend to agree, at a general level, that the respect for rules, procedures, and other formalities is paramount. Bureaucratic formalities mediate interests, facilitate negotiation, and are influenced by the power effects of political mobilization, not simply followed.

TRUSTING AND CONTROLLING INSTITUTIONS

In Scandinavia, people are more involved with the state than in most other areas of the world. In comparative terms, it is striking that this involvement is not generally seen as deeply problematic. The state is not perceived primarily as something they need to avoid and seek protection from, but rather as an essential part of everyone's environment (Trägårdh 2007). The historical roots of this experience go way back, and one of my aims in this book is to trace these roots. The Scandinavian states appear to many observers as somewhat peculiar, and often as quite interesting, apparently due to the mysterious combination of humanism and bureaucratic standardization (Zetterberg 1986). Normally understood as particularly "mature" welfare states (although some rather think of them as overblown), these states are seen as "generous" in the sense that they involve themselves heavily in redistribution (Esping-Andersen 1990, 2002, 2005, 2009). The other side of the coin is the fact that they penetrate deep into most people's lives, and thus undermine their freedom. Yet there is not much evidence to support the expectation that the trust in the state, or the popular support for extending its welfare policies further, is strongly declining (Barth and Moene 2015). Nor is it reasonable to believe that the power of the state, and the heavy responsibility on the parts of people's lives they have taken on, makes people passive, irresponsible, or alienated by bureaucratic invasion, as the inspiration from liberal theory has led many social scientists and others to believe (Sivesing and Selle 2010). In short, the Scandinavian welfare states are still very popular. In light of the financial crisis in 2007, which led to drastic downscaling of welfare spending in many European countries, entrenched deep inequalities, and even a major blow to the hope that the state will actually invest in reducing inequality, this seems remarkable. In Scandinavia, both the belief that the state can be used to solve major collective problems and that its bureaucracy can be freedom generating rather than humiliating, are still quite robust. In comparative terms, this is surprising. How do we explain it?

Hans Magnus Enzensberger, who made a journalistic tour of Sweden and Norway in the 1980s and wrote a book on each country, was at great pains to find out more about this. His attempt seems illustrative of a general trend: he suggested that people's acceptance of the intervening state in all aspects of life is somehow a product of lack of experience (or modernization). In *Swedish Autumn* (1986) he writes:

> Swedish citizens are always willing to comply with their authorities with such naïveté and trust as if the benevolence of the authorities were beyond question…. No doubt this blissful credulity has many causes. The most important of these is probably a lack of experience, for which one can only envy the Swedes. Political powers in this country have since time immemorial refrained from a pastime that has been daily fare in other parts of the world: armed persecution of citizens. (Enzensberger in Zetterberg 1986: 92)

As a result, Enzensberger adds, the institutions of the welfare state can be characterized by a "kind of moral immunity," and are thus able to penetrate "all crevices of daily life, and is regulating the affairs of individuals to an extent that is without comparison in free societies" (Ibid., p. 93). It may not appear as strange or surprising that many commentators, including journalists, anthropologists, and sociologists share Enzensberger's fascination, but the fact that very few of them have tried seriously to understand the phenomenon by actually studying it and trying to explain it, for example, in line with the approach developed by John Barnes, does demand attention.

The political and scholarly discourse on civil society may serve as a point of departure. Since Hegel, via Habermas, American communitarianism, to liberal theories of democratic sustainability, as illustrated by Putnam, Bellah et al., Alexander, and many others, it has been assumed that any liberal democratic regime is in need of some sort of "civil society" that somehow stands apart from "the state" and is able to sustain itself in the form of genuine autonomous "lifeworlds" in the Habermasian sense (Habermas 1987; Trägårdh 2007). The autonomy of civil society is fundamental, the story goes, for cultivating a political culture that reproduces egalitarian social bonds, the motivation to get involved in caring for the common good, and a sense of individual responsibility. Logically this calls for some relatively clearly bounded state that refrains from absorbing and transforming such essential qualities. The perspective may be fruitful for some analytical purposes, but it largely fails to account for some "Scandinavian facts," such as the quite unique growth and viability of voluntary activity, which seems to have been stimulated by state expansion (Sivesind and Selle 2010). Hans Zetterberg, in his contribution to one of the early scholarly explorations of equality in this Northern periphery of Europe, *Norden: The Passion for Equality* (1986), formulates the pessimistic perspective drawn from communitarianism and civil society theory rather bluntly:

> The expansion of social welfare since World War II has largely segregated the consumers of social welfare from normal everyday life. Children are sent to day-nurseries; the unemployed, to retraining centers; the sick, to hospitals; the aged; to old peoples' homes or facilities for the chronically ill. As a rule, wherever welfare policy intervenes, normal social contracts are broken up. (Zetterberg 1986: 95)

However, as Swedish historian Lars Trägårdh has made clear in a series of publications (1997, 2007, 2008), in Scandinavia the idea of "civil society" in their Anglo-American and continental versions appears to some degree at odds with local perceptions. Voluntary activity was never seen as separate from the state, but an integral part of it, and because ideas of freedom became so strongly attached to individual autonomy, public policy and services became essential as a means for realizing both. The classical liberal notion that individual freedom depends on a limited state has been very weak indeed. Trägårdh points out that, paradoxically, extensive public entitlements and services have contributed to generating a radically individualist ethos. Although the population's dependence on the state is a characteristic feature of the Scandinavian welfare states, this dependency has not generally been viewed as deeply problematic. The right to receive state support in the form of economic benefits and public services (which has largely been experienced as conducive to freedom and individual autonomy) seems more highly valued than the freedom from state interference in one's private life, as well as the right to choose not to pay relatively high taxes. One important aspect of this, as the book discusses extensively, and broadly inspired by the work of Trägårdh, is the fact that the institutional arrangements of the Scandinavian welfare states are both *individualizing* and at the same time conducive to the institutionalization of highly collectivist, one-size-fits-all policy solutions. Welfare policies have contributed heavily to reducing individual dependency, not only in the markets, but also in the family, neighborhood, and other social structures.

Summing Up

All stories are told from the vantage point of the social position of those telling them. When I, in this context, try to tell an anthropological story about Norway, and in part Scandinavia at large, it seems to me that I face a double challenge. Anthropology, as the comparative study of society and culture, is the study of the Other par excellence. I am Norwegian, and thus I may not be considered enough of a curious outsider whose references are mainly drawn from another cultural horizon. Moreover, anthropology's subject matter, culture, is not really my main interest in this book. Rather I want to seek a deeper understanding of power, politics, and institutional dynamics as constitutive of social organization, and consequently the main ingredients in what most people seem to think distinguishes Norway and Scandinavia from other European countries, or "the West" for that matter. Why then not stay away from anthropology altogether? My reasons are simple. Anthropology's devotion to difference is, of course, not about the exotic Other, but about taking cultural variation seriously and thinking comparatively. And its analytical tradition and vocabulary are well suited for approaching conventional understandings drawn from within the cultural horizon of the society one describes through a critical lens. Both reasons may have their flaws, but in this book I want to argue that we all may benefit from bringing anthropology closer to the social and institutional context within which anthropologists construct their stories about the Other. By this I mean something very simple: a comparative, or better, relativizing gaze is useful when we try to understand not only how rituals, family life, subjectivity, or informal social relations are enacted, take shape, and produce meaning; it is perhaps even better suited to serve the aim of understanding how people form their lives as they take part in the formal institutions of the modern state.

Although in fact most of their lives are deeply influenced by such institutions, particularly so in a welfare state of the Scandinavian type, anthropologists have mostly either ignored this or described such relationships at arm's length. As a result, to the extent that we actually have "theories" of Scandinavian culture based on solid ethnography, they are based on empirical material drawn from other sources, mainly from informal contexts. Although this certainly is not a problem in itself, I think it may be fruitful to expand the perspective. Such an endeavor of course rests heavily on the valuable perspectives developed by Barth, Barnes, Gullestad, Brox, and others. Let me here briefly emphasize the anthropology of the latter among these, Ottar Brox, and one particular inspiration emerging from it that I think is worth highlighting. In my introduction to this chapter, I discussed the phenomenon of "home blindness," and argued that Norwegian anthropology and the anthropology of Norway have never primarily been about identifying the exotics within. Some of Fredrik Barth's students realized that Barth's analytical emphasis on social process and on the need to identify generating mechanisms that could explain emerging phenomena (his book title, *Cosmologies in the Making*, from 1987 is perhaps the best illustration of this) could be useful for analyzing political change.

One of them, Brox, was himself politically very active, and saw that Barth's analytical framework could be used both academically and practically. When he, while working with his book, *What Is Happening in Northern Norway?* (Hva skjer I Nord-Norge? [1966]), realized that bureaucrats and policy makers were hesitant to embrace his message, he went on to explore anthropologically why that was the case. This was part of a much larger project: to try to understand why state authorities failed (or were simply unwilling) to grasp that their grandiose plans to transform northern Norway into a series of industrial centers did not at all appeal to the coastal population, who utilized the resources available to them in ways that seemed both meaningful, efficient, and sustainable: largely by combining fishing, small-scale agriculture, and seasonal wage labor. One important aspect of his research agenda emerging from this was the ambition to explain how political and bureaucratic institutions conceptualize, represent, and act on the interests of those they are supposed to represent. He developed an acute sensibility to unintended consequences, and his analytical program became largely one of explaining how the mechanisms generating undesirable policy outcomes actually worked, as well as how ideological ideas and programs (and more mundane things, such as self-interest) prevented them from being acknowledged and dealt with (Brox 2016). As noted above, Brox's work constitutes a major influence in this book, and is distinctly "Barthian." However, even though Brox has had a profound influence on political mobilization in Norway, most clearly expressed in the EU membership referendums in 1972 and 1994, his anthropological impact outside Scandinavia has been limited.

Trying to understand how relationships, experiences, and imaginaries are formed as people move "in and out of institutions" seems to me to be an interesting angle to understand life in Scandinavia. I have two main reasons for thinking in such terms: as I have indicated, Scandinavian societies are formalized to an extent that is perhaps never experienced in other parts of the world outside the former Soviet domain; and perhaps more important, as people move in and out of institutions they are not only formed by these institutions; they influence and form them, too. As an anthropologist who has always been mainly inspired by the subject matter of political science and sociology—politics, power, institutions, and social systems—I am somewhat frustrated by the fact that in these disciplines, formal institutions tend largely to be analyzed as though they were either rational unitary agents, or sometimes the opposite: irrational. In both cases, analytical models incorporate imaginary standards to which institutions under study are supposed to conform. My own analytical fascination is rather with institutions as emergent systems of social relations.

REFERENCES

Barnes, J. 1954. Class and Committees in a Norwegian Island Parish. *Human Relations* 7 (1): 39–58.

Barth, Fredrik. 1959. *Political Leadership Among Swat Pathans*. London: Athlone Press.

Barth, Fredrik. 1962. *The Role of the Entrepreneur in Social Change in Northern Norway*. Oslo: Universitetsforlaget.

Barth, Erling, and Kalle Moene. 2015. Political Reinforcement: How Rising Inequality Curbs Manifested Welfare Generosity. *American Political Science* 59 (3): 565–577.

Blom, Jan-Petter. 1969. Ethnic and Cultural Differentiation. In *Ethnic Groups and Boundaries: The Social Organization of Culture Difference*, ed. Fredrik Barth, 75–85. Oslo: Universitetsforlaget.

Brox, Ottar. 1966. *Hva skjer i Nord-Norge? En studie i norsk utkantpolitikk.* Oslo: Pax.

Brox, Ottar. 2016. *På vei mot et postindustrielt klassesamfunn? Om vi vil unngå for store forskjeller i våre barns Norge, er det mye å lære av våre forfedre.* Oslo: Pax.

Dyrvik, S. 1979. *Norsk økonomisk historie 1500-1970*, vol. 1, 1500–1850. Bergen: Universitetsforlaget.

Ebert, Roger. 2005. *No Direction Home: Bob Dylan* (review). Rogerebert.com.

Esping-Andersen, Gösta. 1990. *The Three Worlds of Welfare Capitalism.* Cambridge: Polity Press.

Esping-Andersen, Gösta. 2002. *Why We Need a New Welfare State.* Oxford: Oxford University Press.

Esping-Andersen, Gösta. 2005. Inequality of Incomes and Opportunities. In *The New Egalitarianism*, eds. Giddens, Anthony, and Diamond, Patrick, 8–39. Cambridge and Malden: Polity Press.

Esping-Andersen, Gösta. 2009. *The Incomplete Revolution. Adapting to Women's New Roles.* Cambridge: Polity Press.

Gellner, Ernest. 1983. *Nations and Nationalisms. New Perspectives on the Past.* Oxford: Blackwell.

Gluckman. 1955. The Peace in the Feud. *Past and Present* 8 (1): 1–14.

Gullestad, Marianne. 1984. *Kitchen-Table Society. A Case Study of the Family Life and Friendships of Young Working-Class Mothers in Urban Norway.* Oslo: Universitetsforlaget.

Gullestad, Marianne. 1989. *Kultur og hverdagsliv. På sporet av det moderne Norge.* Oslo: Universitetsforlaget.

Gullestad, Marianne. 1992. Symbolic Fences. In *The Art of Social Relations. Essays on Culture, Social Action and Everyday Life in Modern Norway.* Oslo: Scandinavian University Press.

Gullestad, Marianne. 2001. Likhetens grenser. In *Likhetens paradokser. Antropologiske undersøkelser i det moderne Norge*, eds. Marianne E. Lien, Hilde Lidén & Halvard Vike. Oslo: Universitetsforlaget.

Gullestad, Marianne. 2002. Invisible fences: Egalitarianism, nationalism and racism. *Journal of the Royal Anthropological Institute* 8 (1): 199–226.

Gullestad, Marianne. 2011. Overcoming the division between anthropology «at home» and «abroad». Marianne Gullestad intervjuet av Marianne Lien og Marit Melhuus. *Norsk antropologisk tidsskrift* 22 (02): 134–143.

Habermas, Jürgen. 1987. *The Theory of Communicative Action*, vol. I-II. Boston: Beacon Press.

Holtedahl, Lisbeth. 1986. *Hva mutter gjør er alltid riktig. Om å være kvinne og mann i en nordnorsk bygd i 1970-årene.* Oslo: Universitetsforlaget.

Jackson, Anthony (ed.). 1987. *Anthropology at Home*. New York: Tavistock/Methuen.

Jørgensen, Rikke E. 2017. *"Vi er altid faldet mellem flere stole"*. *Socialøkonomi og social virksomhed "betwixt and between"*. PhD thesis. Doctoral School of People and Technology, Roskilde.

Rudie, Ingrid (ed.). 1984. *Myk start – hard landing. Om forvaltning av kjønnsidentitet i en endringsprosess*. Oslo: Universitetsforlaget.

Sivesind, Karl Henrik, and Per Selle. 2010. Civil Society in the Nordic Countries: Between Displacement and Vitality. In *Nordic Associations in a European Perspective*, ed. Henrik Stenius and Risto Alapuro. Baden-Baden: Nomos.

Sørensen, Øystein, and Bo Stråth. 1997. *The Cultural Construction of Norden*. Oslo: Scandinavian University Press.

Sørhaug, Hans Christian 1986. Totemisme på norsk—betraktninger om det norske sosialdemokratiets vesen. In *Den norske væremåten*, eds. Klausen, Arne Martin, 61–88. Oslo: Da Capo.

Stenius, Henrik 2010: Nordic Associational Life in a European and an Inter-Nordic Perspective. In *Nordic Associations in a European Perspective*, ed. Stenius, Henrik and Alapuro, Risto. Baden-Baden: Nomos.

Strathern, Marilyn. 1987. The limits of auto-anthropology. In *Anthropology at Home*, ed. Anthony Jackson, 16–37. New York: Tavistock/Methuen.

Sundt, Eilert. 2006. *Om sædeligheds-tilstanden i Norge*. Oslo: Bokklubben.

Sundt, Eilert. (1817–1875) 2010. *Om sædeligheds-tilstanden i Norge*. Oslo: Bokklubben.

Trägårdh, Lars 1997. Statist Individualism. On the Culturality of the Nordic Welfare State. In *The Cultural Construction of Norden*, eds. Sørensen, Øystein, and Bo Stråth, 253–285. Oslo: Scandinavian University Press.

Trägårdh, Lars. 2007. The "Civil Society" Debate in Sweden: The Welfare State Challenged. In *State and Civil Society in Northern Europe. The Swedish Model reconsidered*, ed. Lars Trägårdh, 9–37. New York: Berghahn Books.

Trägårdh, Lars. 2008. Det civila samhällets karriär som vetenskapligt och politiskt begrepp i Sverige, *Tidskrift for samfunnsforskning* 49 (4): 575–594.

Zetterberg, Hans L. 1986. The Rational Humanitarians. In *Norden—The Passion for Equality*, ed. Stephen R. Graubard, 79–97. Oslo: Norwegian University Press.

CHAPTER 3

The Politics of Universalism

WELFARE POLITICS IN SKIEN MUNICIPALITY

In the Skien municipality, as in local politics in Norway in general, welfare policy (along with primary education), and the budget problems related to it constitute major issues and concerns, and loom larger in local public debate than any other issue. In the fall of 1993, the Municipal Assembly voted on a general budget that, as it turned out, would involve serious cutbacks in the Health and Welfare Department. This became a big challenge for the Health and Welfare Committee, the political body that serves as the executive body of the Municipal Assembly and the Municipal Council. In October that fall, a clear and deep sense of crisis had developed among the political representatives in the committee. The committee requested the Municipal Council to make adjustments and reduce or abolish the cuts, but with no success. As a result, the committee decided to reject the budget proposal. Under dramatic circumstances the elected leader of the committee declared on behalf of all the political representatives that they were ready to *ta opp kampen med elitepolitikere i alle partier* ("fight elite politicians in all parties"). This rebellious strategy was experienced by the committee members as a breakthrough. It remedied their sense of having become hostages of an unrealistic budget policy on the part of the Council, which had implemented the general

© The Author(s) 2018   51
H. Vike, *Politics and Bureaucracy in the Norwegian Welfare State*,
Approaches to Social Inequality and Difference,
https://doi.org/10.1007/978-3-319-64137-9_3

guidelines made by the Assembly. It created some problems, too, the most basic among which was that the committee members, in their capacity as members of the Assembly, had voted for the budget guidelines. Thus they found themselves in a role dilemma.

The formal organization of the municipal political institutions in Skien is not parliamentary. The Municipal Assembly is the superior body and constituted of proportional representation. The Municipal Council serves as a preparatory forum and mirrors the distribution of political power as expressed by the Assembly, but through delegation the Council has also been endowed with independent power in some matters. Because all the major parties are represented in the Council, political discourse is not organized by an opposition between the government and the opposition. As a consequence political tensions are often channeled towards several other arenas such as the political parties and between different levels in the decision-making hierarchy. The relationship between *hovedutvalgene* ("the major committees," of which there are three: Health and Welfare, Education and Culture, and Infrastructure), which have some independent decision-making power but which, in all major issues are responsible to the Council and the Assembly, and the Council, on the other hand, is particularly relevant. This relationship is often portrayed as one between "grassroots" and "elite politicians," although the two categories include people who are often very close (and members of the same party). Indeed, most politicians are represented at both levels.

In other words, the struggle against the local political elite during the fall of 1993 cut across all traditional political cleavages. Arguing that the budget would make it impossible to meet the needs of the population, the committee signaled that the whole issue was really not about budgets and figures but a matter of moral responsibility. The rebellion was thus justified by reference to the needs of *de svake gruppene i samfunnet* ("the weak ones in society"), particularly the elderly, the disabled, refugees, and people on social welfare. The rebellion was very emotional and passionate. The members of the committee expressed great relief at the fact that the decision to reject the Council's budget proposal was unanimous. One of the Labour Party representatives placed his hand on his heart and told me that, at last, the harmony between his mind and body was resurrected.

During the fall of 1993, I took part in various party meetings and spoke with many local politicians about these matters. Here I present some of the key issues that were debated during that period, and separate the chain of events into three phases. I show how the discussions gradually became transformed from a narrow budget debate into one that concerned the principles of welfare policy in general, the meaning of the welfare state, and what municipal responsibility is about.

PHASE 1: THE POLITICS OF MORALISM

The social welfare issue was presented during the spring of 1993 and was motivated by the need to save money. The proposition forwarded by the municipal administration to the HW committee was to reduce welfare payments to unemployed people who, because of additional problems, were unlikely to obtain jobs. For many years, the municipality had struggled to reduce the social welfare budget, the "explosion" of which seemed to have become an annual phenomenon, due to what was commonly called "unrealistic budgeting." Because the criteria for supporting welfare clients economically were not clearly defined, as the central state had issued guidelines that, if followed, would involve higher expenses than what Skien municipality could carry, attempts to establish better control over the local budget had proved to have little effect.

Because of high unemployment rates during the early 1990s, the number of people applying for welfare support rose. A main argument for the need to reduce municipal expenses was that it was necessary to bring the standard in line with that of the neighboring municipalities, where payments were somewhat lower. Some politicians worried that many of Skien's clients were "welfare migrants" from neighboring municipalities. Most important, however, was the need to save money and to eliminate misappropriations of welfare funds. The underlying premise was that implementing budgetary constraints did not represent a fundamental break with the idea that everyone, including the unemployed and those experiencing various social problems, had access to material and social welfare. The issue evoked heated debate that revolved around this underlying premise.

The conflicting definitions developed in the committee were predicated upon diverging interpretations of the moral basis of this issue: that is, should entitlement be based on moral or economic criteria? G. Eidskog, the leading Socialist Party representative, was the first to develop the moral argument. Interestingly, however, the nature of the problems faced by social clients (whether they were really "weak") was only a secondary theme in the early phase of the discussion. He did not argue that the reduction of payments would increase the vulnerability of these people, but rather that the politicians themselves were not in a moral position to make such a move. He referred to the recent positive developments in the credit market, which had given most people, "people like us," he emphasized, more money. "This," he said, "is a question of morality. One cannot reduce welfare benefits to people who haven't received what *we've* got." Furthermore, he added the more practical argument that even though one might craft a majority behind the proposal, it would not help, because the clients are only moved around from one municipal budget post to another anyway. "Basically, this is manipulating with numbers," he pointed out.

Everyone who supported the proposal to reduce the municipal budget underscored that it was really against their will to do so. They insisted that in the last analysis, they really had no choice. J. Sandvik, for instance, who spoke on behalf of the Labour Party (who had three representatives on the committee), said that although he was sympathetic to Eidskog's argument, it was necessary to consider more than this case alone. To him, *helheten* ("the whole picture"), that is, the budget balance, was crucial.

The leading conservative representative, W. Norheim, also took issue with Eidskog's argument that the proposal would result in nothing but "manipulation with numbers." She pointed out that the problem was "real" and that the committee was *pålagt* ("forced") by higher authorities (the Council) to make this decision. She added that the experience of going through hard times is not limited to welfare clients: "Other people are struggling too. Some have to sell their houses and buy smaller apartments." Sandvik protested against this approach and told her that to sell a house worth millions is a perfectly reasonable thing to do, but that this is really something wholly different from experiencing real economic problems, as unemployed and welfare clients in fact do. Norheim replied by saying that "I am actually talking about people like you and me." The debate was concluded by the KRF (Christian Democratic Party) representative, who reformulated the overall need to save money as follows: "We have to put our efforts together in order to save ... Eidskog is concerned about social welfare, and that's good, but we have to save money." Sandvik supported this argument and emphasized once again that the Committee was forced to save. "Besides," he added, "there are *many* weak groups, and Eidskog has talked about other groups before." By this statement, Sandvik referred to the alleged tendency among Socialist Party representatives to be too generous in their welfare policy orientation, thus leaving the municipality with too great a responsibility.

During this first phase of the controversy, the politicians established two different frames of reference. Both related to alternative and conflicting constructions of the municipality's responsibility in the area of social welfare. The Socialist Party representative presented the case as one involving the very idea of the welfare state's (or the municipality's) responsibility towards the weak. His argument accentuated what we may call a hierarchical understanding (Kapferer 1988) of the welfare state and municipality. According to this understanding, the whole has priority over its parts and constitutes a moral entity in itself. The welfare state is understood as a moral entity whose integrity depends on how the weak in society are treated. This morality is the core reference point from which politicians who identify with this position proceed. The opponents in this case chose not to apply this understanding, and saw themselves mainly as responsible agents whose loyalty towards the municipal organization was expressed through budget discipline.

Both understandings constituted possible, and potentially legitimate, options for the politicians. However, they saw both as problematic. The traditional hierarchical option connecting the welfare of marginal clients to the integrity of the welfare state was increasingly experienced as more or less naïve and simplistic because clients could no longer simply be expected to be of the deserving kind. In addition, due to economic scarcity the municipality could no longer serve unconditionally as a compensatory device and reach out to solve problems on everyone's behalf. Rather, as a local politician, one is responsible for the task of guarding municipal boundaries from the surrounding environment, particularly from free-riders. On the other hand, all the members of the committee agreed that the task of strengthening the welfare society by securing decent living conditions for everyone was paramount. As we show later, those "elite politicians" and leading administrators who argued the strongest for limiting municipal costs were, most of the time, the primary targets of moral criticism.

Phase 2: Staging a Rebellion

Later the same fall the budget discussions became more difficult and tense. In the period prior to the final budget debate, shortly after the welfare issue had been discussed in the HW committee, it was commonly agreed that the task would be a tough one. Within the proposed budget, it seemed impossible to satisfy the increasing demands of the public. This increase was mainly due to the rising number of elderly people who would be in need of municipal care in the near future. The HW director (the administrative leader of the department) said: "This development does not follow the budget at all." In the eyes of administrative personnel and politicians alike, the amount and quality of services would—if nothing were done—have to be reduced. Therefore, the first question was how to establish priorities within the budget, and the second was concerned with whether the committee should request the Assembly to grant more money. The background material presented to the politicians was in one sense clear-cut. It described possible moves that could be made in order to maintain the budget balance and the responsibility towards the Assembly, represented by the *rådmannen* (the chief administrator of the municipality). The HW director's primary loyalty is towards the *rådmannen*, and thus the background material was shaped by the imperative to maintain budget balance. It said little in terms of the consequences for the quality of service. However, the message from the service-providing units and employees conveyed a strong sense of crisis. In the reports they had provided it was argued that it was not possible to meet the municipalities' responsibility towards its users, and asked the politicians to take responsibility for quality reductions.

Therefore, the HW director was caught in a difficult role dilemma, as she had to choose between budget loyalty and the professional advice provided by the units. Hence, at the outset of the debate, she had to clarify to the politicians that although it was an uncomfortable situation for her, her loyalty to her administrative superior was paramount. She told the political representatives in the committee that "I understand you perfectly well, but I have to act on behalf of the *rådmannen*. If you want larger budgets, you have to work on a broader basis and discuss it in your parties." As we show later, her choice of loyalty gave rise to strong disagreements at a later stage of the process, because it turned out that it conflicted with the politicians' solution to their own dilemma. This solution was to reject the budget proposal for which they themselves, in their capacity as members of the Municipal Assembly, were formally responsible. This generated a perspective and a line of argument radically different from the ones that dominated the debate on welfare payments. As the representatives entered the room where the meeting was held, they all expressed a sense of relief that contrasted strongly with the serious concern expressed in their faces only a few days earlier. The issue had been discussed informally prior to the meeting and a basic consensus had been achieved. The budget meeting commenced with a presentation of the consensus. Norheim opened this part of the meeting in the following fashion.

> Budget discussions are seldom happy occasions. I have been a part of this for six years, and there [have] been cutbacks all the time. We are struggling and suffering, and we are now in the process of cutting away the rest. Large groups in the municipality are unable to meet their needs. We are caught in a swamp, and we cannot take responsibility for this situation. The situation for the elderly is telling: we need twenty-three million kroner and have to cut away four million. It is often said that politicians are unwilling to take responsibility. We do take responsibility for the clients; it is towards them we now turn our focus. We know more about the problem than other politicians do, and they ought to listen more closely to us. All parties agree with this. It was a good experience (coming to an agreement prior to the current meeting, HV), in fact, and there was really no controversy. We have reached the limit! We are not interested in participating in the suffering any more. We will never be able to get out of this mess if we don't say stop now!

This position set the stage for the rest of the meeting. Most importantly, it defined the kind of loyalty that was to count as fundamental: not to the administration and the Assembly, but the clients. Once this was done, the definition of responsibility followed more or less automatically. The other speakers sought to add more substance and legitimacy to the version already presented by Norheim, and the meeting was really not characterized by political discussion at all, but rather by a series of more or less repetitive presentations of the same point of view. C. Eng formulated his version of the consensus in this way:

> After having participated in the preliminary discussions my mind was much lighter. This has been a plague for a long time.... This is a signal to the political establishment that it must dare to take responsibility for our sector and prioritize human values. The pressure on our employees is intolerable. We have been running from catastrophe to catastrophe and from media coverage to media coverage.

Eng's presentation further stressed the need for doing something dramatic to counteract the existing situation. Although all the protagonists in the debate saw the need to save money as "natural" and in harmony with "reality," in this situation they viewed the budget as an obstacle to maintaining moral integrity. This made the committee members see their own protest against the budget as a heroic act. Eng stressed that "Now we have to fight against elite politicians in all parties." Eidskog followed him saying, "We agree roughly on how we want to make the priorities. We all have to fight. If they don't understand it, it is us who have failed. We are talking about real human destinies here." The sense of relief thus created was most clearly enunciated by B. Asbjørnsen, one of the three Labor Party representatives, who said that "This feels so good, because now the committee speaks as one. In our sector people may in fact be dying, but now we want no more of this!" Later, in the break and over a cup of coffee, he told me and the others present that at last he was able to "craft policies with the mind and the body on behalf of those for whom we are responsible." He placed his hand gently on his stomach to illustrate how well he felt.

However, even though the committee was unanimous and characterized by a strong sense of relief, one politician, A. Langset, injected a tiny dose of doubt at the meeting. He warned the others against the tendency to underestimate other politicians and indicated that perhaps the chosen line of action was not in harmony with the idea of responsibility at all:

> We are in a position where we have to point out that we cannot afford everything we want. Perhaps we should have been awake a little earlier, but in Skien we have seen who's joining the protest marches. But don't underestimate our political colleagues. They know how things are, and they know it from the newspapers too.

The reference to the protest marches was a comment on popular participation in Skien. Prior to the budget debate, the politicians had witnessed a series of protest marches involving teachers, school children, and parents protesting against cutbacks in the school budget. Many politicians thought that these people were really "among the resourceful ones," an interest group using its strength to put pressure on politicians and, thus, indirectly threatening the interests of those who were vulnerable in a more genuine sense. He added that it had disappointed him to observe that people would demand more money so bluntly, without considering the municipalities' difficult financial situation.

During the break, I talked with one of the subdepartment leaders, the head of the social services, who informally admitted that he felt greatly relieved. The situation prior to the current meeting had put him *i et forfærdelig rolledilemma* ("in a terrible role dilemma"), due to the collision between his own professional conscience and responsibility towards his subordinates and clients, on the one hand, and his formal loyalty. The decision that just had been made by the politicians removed this dilemma. However, the us/them construction established in the committee meeting was, as indicated above, not complete. Everybody knew that the director felt ill at ease with the protest, which conflicted with the interests of the *rådmannen*. Eidskog was particularly aware of this, and stated at the end of the budget session, "I expect that the administration is loyal towards the politicians and that it doesn't *stå skolerett* ("subordinate itself") to the will of the *rådmannen*."

Although this meeting involved the most dramatic political decision I witnessed during my fieldwork in Skien, it reflected a tension that permeated most issues. In this particular case, the politicians rejected the authoritative definition of budget responsibility; in fact, it put an end to the budgetary process in the form in which it was intended, and established a moral opposition between loyalty and the municipalities' responsibility to provide services. Moreover, as noted above, it introduced an alternative political cleavage between the "grassroots" and what became categorized as "the elite politicians."

In this phase, the entire committee chose to apply the understanding promoted by the Socialist Party representative in the first phase, the very same type of understanding its members, at that time, portrayed as naïve and simplistic. Although the two cases described in Phases 1 and 2 were virtually identical, the representatives had radically changed their opinion over time. By Phase 2 all the representatives were apparently convinced that any other path of action would have been immoral. This time, neither the categorical construction of "the weak ones in society" nor municipal responsibility gave rise to ambivalence and contradictions. The moral pathos involved in the making of consensus relieved the committee members of a major dilemma and harmonized their deeply felt political conviction with action. The dilemma was, at least temporarily, shifted to the administrative director (who saw herself as responsible for the *rådmannen* and, ultimately, the Assembly), and had been transformed. As shown below, what in this context was a political problem became a classical administrative question of loyalty in the next.

PHASE 3: CONTESTING LOYALTY

One week later, the committee came together to discuss the matter once again. The premise for the discussion was to follow the decision made the week before and back it up with more background material on how much money the sector would need in order to maintain municipal health and welfare services at an *akseptabelt nivå* ("acceptable level"). In the previous meeting, the administration had been assigned the task of preparing this material as quickly as possible. In accordance with the new political strategy, the politicians repeated and intensified their arguments developed in Phase 2, and emphasized even more strongly the idea that health and welfare policies are special because they involve human beings in more direct ways than is the case in other policy areas.

> However, the meeting turned out to be a major setback, and in what follows we see why. It turned out that the material that the political representatives had requested the week before had in fact not been prepared. Norheim expressed her disappointment in these terms: "Here we go again. This is serious; because we are dealing with living human beings. ... The budget is immoral and unethical. I use strong words, but I really mean it. I had hoped that other politicians would listen to us.

In this context "other politicians" connoted "elite politicians in all parties" against whom she wanted the committee to mobilize and fight. Strictly denotatively, "other politicians" primarily referred to the Plan and Economy Committee (PEC), which served as a preparatory forum for the Council, and which consisted of two Labor Party representatives and one from each of the other parties (except from the Liberal Party). Norheim felt that the absence of the supporting material they had requested had something to do with a lack of support from the Plan and Economy Committee. The HW director had already indicated this at the beginning of the meeting. She had pointed out that she was not sure whether everyone understood what "the new budget process," as it was commonly called at the time, really meant. In short, according to the director the new procedure was simply an adjustment to the new Municipal Law, which had been issued some years before and was about to be implemented throughout the country. The official purpose of this new law was to provide room for a more active role on the part of the politicians at the cost of the administration in the preparatory phase of the budgetary process. Therefore, this year it was the Council and not the *rådmannen* who presented the budget proposal. The director's statement was a careful attempt to explain that her own, and supposedly the committee's, role was to follow the political guidelines which were formulated by the Council. To provide the new material and pursue this new path of action would conflict with these guidelines, she argued.

Norheim's frustration over the fact that the material wasn't there seemed to be shared by everyone present, but no one was really sure how to articulate it. Hence, Sandvik chose to follow Norheim's reasoning in her attack on other politicians and said, "Other politicians say that we should not involve our emotions in what we're doing, and I'm tired of that. Emotions have to be involved. We want to support those who need it the most." Eng also supported this view but added that he was disappointed that he hadn't received the professional, administrative help he had hoped for, "… in order to provide a description of reality which could make the situation more visible," he said. He needed that because, as he put it, it was difficult to have to prepare oneself for *ens egen dødsdom* ("one's own death sentence"). This comment opened the way for a clearer delineation of the director's standpoint, which she had presented in relatively careful terms at the beginning of the meeting. She said that the whole matter is a difficult one because "it really is about your relationship to other politicians." In the eyes of the political representatives in the committee, this was an extremely provoking statement, and D. Eide, one of the two Socialist Party representatives, rather aggressively asked: "Stop me if I'm wrong, but I thought we were all riding the same horse and had the same goal. To whom are you loyal?" To this question, the director sharpened her original statement, explaining that the political responsibility was theirs, whereas her loyalty had to be towards the *rådmannen*, whose main responsibility is to stick to the general budget guidelines made earlier by the Assembly. The logical outcome for the committee members, then, would be to make a greater political effort at an earlier stage of the budget process. The implication of this statement was, of course, that the politicians were now really protesting against decisions made by themselves. The situation was very hostile and uncomfortable and became even more so when Eng responded by confronting all the director's deputies by asking them, "To whom are *you* loyal?" Formally, their personal views were, of course, irrelevant, and their professional advice—which was unambiguous and in perfect harmony with the committee's position at the last meeting—had clearly been reformulated and undermined by the director. Hence, they felt that they could say nothing, just sit there and hope to escape the terror of being caught in a political-bureaucratic crossfire. Although clearly the politicians were very disappointed, they did little except repeat their frustration and protests. As it turned out, the tension further stimulated the sense of relief and unconditional commitment to the oppositional strategy that had been developed the previous week. T. Asbjørnsen formulated this feeling as follows.

> Now I *banner i kjerka* ("swear in the church") and say what I feel. I have often wondered if I participate in politics for the wrong reasons. People say that we're not involved in politics but rather in administration. Is the criterion for participating that you must be an accountant or a cashier?

Norheim's earlier comment also indicated that the director's argument was not regarded as convincing. She continued to talk about the Council as "other politicians": "I feel like a fender. I have the sense that someone is more concerned with dealing with numbers than with solving problems."

It soon became clear however, that the director's argument that the administration was caught in a conflict of interest that was political and should be treated as such, made the politicians give up. It is relevant to note here that the director's tough approach created a very strong and widespread frustration among the administrative staff. In conversations with me many of them said that they felt forced to carry out the good intentions on behalf of the politicians while, at the same time, being economically "strangled," as one of them put it. This is why the conflict of interest between the director and her deputies occurred in the meeting, shown by the incident when she refused to let them speak, even when confronted directly by the politicians' questions. Their hope was clearly that the rebellion would contribute to solving their basic dilemma: the obligation to provide welfare services on a universal basis without the necessary resources, and at the same time carry the responsibility for inadequate services. The committee's oppositional strategy made them optimistic because they hoped it would bring some degree of consistency between political ambitions and resources.

And although they clearly felt that the director had unnecessarily humiliated them in front of the politicians, they respected her argument that the politicians should stay away from making the administration a political ally, and in part a tool, in their struggle against the Assembly, or "elite politicians."

INTERPRETATIONS

As we have seen, the controversy leading to the welfare policy rebellion in Skien in 1993 started out as a discussion of the legitimacy of needs among welfare clients. As it appeared from this initial debate, a unitary and shared "ideology of universalism" was not something the committee representatives shared. As the case demonstrates, they (or at least several among them) were ready to question whether welfare clients really deserved what they received, and some were quite willing to deal with principles of welfare policy as relative to budget restraints. However, as this problem became encompassed by larger questions pertaining to the elderly population in particular, things changed. Whether this happened because the elderly serve as the prototype of legitimate needs, or rather because the scale of the whole issue became a wholly different one, is not clear. However, what did become unambiguously clear was that the representatives increasingly came to see themselves as representatives of the local community and "the weak groups," rather as guardians of scarce budgets. This identity was institutionally readily available to them, and until this point they seemed to have seen themselves as both representatives of "the weak groups" vis-à-vis the municipality and representatives of the municipality vis-à-vis the same groups, often contextually migrating between them. This would indicate that they were not caught in some powerful "hegemonic discourse," but rather evaluated pragmatically the options available to them (Vike 2012).

Furthermore, it appeared to me, as an observer, that in 1993 these politicians had not yet become accustomed to the practice of delegating to the Assembly, and its extension the Council and the Plan and Economy Committee, a decisive say in defining budgetary allocations to the sectors. It seemed to me that they rather saw the budget proposal as a kind of advice, which it had previously been. That was why, I further assume, they didn't pay much attention to their own role dilemma and the fact that they were, formally speaking, themselves among the "elite politicians" against whom they rebelled. Therefore,

they were quite provoked when they realized that they were faced
with a dictate, and that they were forced, as they themselves saw it, to
choose between serving as the loyal servants of the local elites or represent the population.

The creation of mutual solidarity among the representatives of the
committee was surely not intended purely as a rhetorical signal. In their
experience, the establishment of ad hoc horizontal solidarity related to
specific political issues was a useful mechanism that had proved successful many times before. As far as I could grasp, it was an important part
of the ordinary, both formal and informal control of elites who, once
placed in key positions, tended to seek better control and thus be better equipped to use limited resources the best way possible, according
to what they often called "the whole picture." The members of the
committee were used to challenging this particular construction of the
whole picture, and criticized political leaders more or less continuously
for not realizing that the whole picture has to be based on real experience with those the municipality is set to serve. Such alliances would
often cut across the boundaries between politics and bureaucracy, as well
as between bureaucratic layers and functions. As we saw, the committee members asked the subdepartment leaders to whom they were loyal,
and initially they expected the director to be a part of the alliance. In
between the meetings, several of the most active committee members
were busy creating alliances outside the municipal organizations, and
they used their key positions in networks of voluntary organizations and
unions to achieve this. The conservative representative was a nurse and a
very active member of the local historical society; in addition, she had for
several years served as perhaps the most important spokesperson of both
the local unions (in the HW sector) and the users' organizations. The
two representatives from the Labour Party were also centrally placed in
local associational life, both within the sector but also in sports organizations and in the myriad low church congregations existing in Skien.
Moreover, both were important spokespersons for the backbenchers
in the Assembly and the local branches of the Labour Party, of which
there were five very active ones in the municipality. The Progress Party
representative was not equally well equipped with such organizational
resources, but he had achieved considerable respect in all political parties, as he was among the most active of the local politicians and cultivated intimate ties to local protest groups that were less well organized
than the traditional organizations. The socialist was a well-respected

and outspoken rector of a secondary school in Skien, and his credibility among people on the left was considerable.

It should be added to this that these politicians also knew very well that welfare policy is the most important domain of politics in Skien (as well as in most other Norwegian municipalities), and that their rebellion would mobilize much support in the local media. It was also part of common knowledge that the central state, through the directorates, the regional governor, and other agencies, continuously criticized municipalities for failing to provide welfare services in accordance with quality standards and accessibility. This provided politicians with powerful tools with which they might legitimately challenge budget orthodoxy, at least up to a point. Although, unsurprisingly, the main policy of any government is to secure that expenses are brought under control, not that needs are in fact met, universalism rests on a strong ideological and moral ethos. In principle, this means that the politics of the welfare state often become directly related to questions of the quality and accessibility of service. When it is revealed that quality and coverage are insufficient, service providers and their allies may seize the opportunity to politicize the discrepancy between intentions/ambitions/rights and the realities on the ground, and anchor their arguments in the language of formal citizen rights. This is why, prior to the last meeting in the committee, the director had to prevent her deputies from presenting the requested material. Although such battles are very hard to win, my point here is that the municipal institution constitutes a political and bureaucratic arena where alliances that are mobilized around them in fact become a real force and cannot simply be ignored. In my view, it is hard to overestimate the structural contradiction generated by the combination of universalism and managerial hierarchical government. In principle, universalism stimulates a needs-driven, potentially very costly form of welfare policy that makes the ambition to maintain managerial and financial control more or less unrealistic. As I have tried to show, one decisive factor influencing the effect of this contradiction is the strength of those arenas where people may create horizontal alliances. In 1993, such alliances did have a direct bearing on how the institutions of the state made their priorities.

The rebellion may thus be understood as a conventional form of political contention, and an organizational resource to be used as a way of circumventing the arguments and the power of local elites. The budget proposal had in fact been forwarded through a formal process in all political parties. Political leaders, especially those holding seats in the Council, had been convinced (by the *rådmannen*) that "the whole picture" demanded budget discipline in a more literal sense, and they had won a majority in their respective parties. In this context, political backbenchers were on the defensive due to their lack of insight into budget technicalities; they mostly relied on their ability to mobilize support for fighting battles over again in *other* contexts, arguing that new information had become known, and discussions that were more thorough were needed.

Also, and with special reference to the question of loyalty discussed in the process, the rebellion may be interpreted as a kind of historical moment taking place within the context of a larger process of welfare state transformation. As we saw, the director had spoken to the *rådmannen* and the leading politicians about what "the new" budget process would mean. When she rejected providing the information demanded by the committee, the committee members were surprised, even shocked. They seemed to feel that they had been given a role much like that of the subdepartment leaders: loyal followers of an administrative boss. In this way, they were cut off from taking part in alliances that transcended institutional boundaries and undermined administrative loyalty in the strict sense. The same thing happened to the political representatives on the committee, who had now become incorporated in the municipal administrative hierarchy as individuals.

Let me point out here that in my ethnographic work in municipal worlds since the 1990s, I have observed a radical decline in challenges to administrative authority and its right to set the terms for how to govern a municipality in line with standards established by the central state. As a consequence, a drastic reduction in the moral potential for resistance inherent in political ambitions and state guarantees that seek to secure universal welfare (in concrete terms: quality and accessibility) is taking place. In terms of the perspective on gift giving and the reproduction of the relative autonomy of moral–political spheres outlined in Chap. 1, we see here a relatively clear-cut illustration of how one important mechanism of horizontal political solidarity is in part undermined by a hierarchical system of command based on personal loyalty, disguised as budget discipline and administrative order. Political resistance of the type described above has largely become synonymous with breaching proper administrative procedure. As a consequence, the very idea of mobilizing horizontally to protect the quality of service has increasingly become unrealistic, and thus harder to imagine. In analytical terms, this suggests that welfare state universalism is not to be seen primarily as an ideological category, despite the fact that the electoral success of any political party depends on keeping it high on the agenda. As the case indicates, universalism seems rather to depend on particular forms of political and bureaucratic representation that enables institutional actors to act collectively on the basis of some identity other than simple loyalty, hierarchically defined and codified as straightforward realism and budget discipline. What I have called the low level of gravity state enables actors to imagine identities and paths of action other than what the hierarchical chain of command deems necessary, natural, rational, and realistic.

As noted, the case may be seen in light of my discussion of the logics of gift giving in Chap. 1. The politics of mutual support underlying the "solidarity" that developed among the committee members involved, as I understand it in these terms, acknowledging each other's membership in a community of representatives. Because everyone knew that this identity was situational, the mutual recognition and sense of dignity they developed was conditional and not a claim to loyalty. As a community of members they came to see themselves as morally obliged to represent what they saw as the common view among people in the wider community. When the director rejected respecting their instruction to provide the documentation they wanted, they appeared shocked and felt that their autonomy both as politicians/representatives and moral persons was invaded. "The moral sphere" within which they had been accustomed to operate, which was driven by the symmetrical exchange of recognition and, on the part of each individual member, an autonomous choice to join, had seemingly become irrelevant (and perhaps even pathetic) and substituted with a chain of administrative command based on personal loyalty. As we saw, the committee members were used to being able to use political consensus to take control over the sector, through instructing or seeking the support of the director and encouraging the subdepartment leaders to join the alliance, thus breaking up the municipal administrative system and involving it in political contention and negotiation. This, as I see it, enabled them to act on what I have called the politics of universalism. By this I do not refer to a clear-cut ideology or policy strategy, but to the simple fact that this specific form of political action made it possible to mobilize political power, through the representative chain, to secure the interests of those who were likely to be hit by the effects of cutbacks and resist "the social production of indifference" (Herzfeld 1992).

REFERENCES

Herzfeld, Michael. 1992. *The Social Production of Indifference. Exploring the Symbolic Roots of Western Bureaucracy.* Chicago: The University of Chicago Press.

Kapferer, Bruce. 1988. *Legends of People, Myths of State. Violence, Intolerance and Political Culture in Sri Lanka and Australia.* Washington: Smithsonian Institution Press.

Vike, Halvard. 2012. Varianter av Vest-europeiske Statsformasjoner–Utkast til en Historisk Antropologi. *Norsk Antropologisk Tidsskrift* 23 (2): 126–142.

CHAPTER 4

The Welfare State and the Possibility of Solidarity

THE POLITICS OF SOLIDARITY

Peter Baldwin, in his path-breaking book, *The Politics of Social Solidarity–Class Bases of the European Welfare State 1875–1975* (1990), is concerned with the question of how, in modern democratic states, horizontal ties are built, and how they are translated into political power. Also, as the title indicates, he is interested in and tries to explain how this, in Europe, generated different welfare state models. The short story is, to simplify Baldwin's complex analysis, that although the labor movement was a crucial factor throughout Europe in challenging hierarchy, privilege, clientelism/patrimonialism, and elitism as foundational principles in political life and partly substituting them with horizontal social ties, that was never enough. Historical experience strongly suggests that in order to change the tables, much broader alliances were needed.

In Scandinavia, two emergent properties of political modernization stand out as unique in a European context. The farming population, which John Barnes in his *Class and Committees in a Norwegian Island Parish* (1954) labeled "part-time peasants" (see Chap. 2), were active "politicians" and had been so for a long time. In Sweden, yeoman farmers were represented in the Diet from the sixteenth century onwards, and in Norway they had been politically active in various municipal contexts before the municipal law in 1837 (Stenius 2010). "The politics of social

© The Author(s) 2018
H. Vike, *Politics and Bureaucracy in the Norwegian Welfare State,*
Approaches to Social Inequality and Difference,
https://doi.org/10.1007/978-3-319-64137-9_4

solidarity," in Baldwin's terms, was already well established when the labor movement achieved political influence in the early twentieth century. Even though political representation was mainly local, it brought the farming population in direct contact with the state apparatus (as opposed to local feudal lords). Scandinavian peasant-farmers were major agents in the transformation of the old, hierarchical, and largely antidemocratic political order prevailing up to the turn of the century (Sørensen and Stråth 1997). During the nineteenth century, they formed political movements that exerted considerable influence on the state regimes, and established politically successful alliances with liberal elites aspiring to parliamentary influence (Sejersted 2005). These alliances in turn became fundamental in constructing the ideological and political basis for both democratic reforms and state policy, especially economic policies and welfare policies. When the labor movements and the social democratic parties in Sweden, Denmark, and Norway, respectively, achieved parliamentary hegemony from the 1930s onwards, they largely extended a political agenda that was originally developed by this agrarian–liberal alliance. Although the labor movement and the agrarian population were ideological antagonists, especially during the times of economic crisis and the growth of fascist sensibilities in the early twentieth century, in all three countries they joined forces in the 1930s and made it possible for the Social Democrats to assume governmental power (Arter 2008).

The second important point in Baldwin's analysis of the possibility of horizontal ties to be transformed into political power and, ultimately, comprehensive policies of redistribution, concerns the interests of the middle classes. Although a broad and thus crude generalization, it seems safe to say that comprehensive policies of redistribution depend on a majority of a (national) population seeing such policies not only sympathetically as "generous" to the poor and marginalized, but serving their own interests as well. We now know that the success of any ambitious welfare state seems to rest on precisely this type of policy framework (Rothstein 2011; Moene and Barth 2015). No European welfare state that was not oriented towards universalism in the first place has in fact survived, and in the few countries that followed the path of universalism to start with (The Netherlands, Britain, France, and to some extent Germany) the attractiveness of the welfare agenda has in effect been undermined. This all seems to go back to Baldwin's insight, namely that the class dynamics shaping the forming of organized political interests do not alone explain variations of welfare state experiments in Europe. The alliances that were formed between classes also played a crucial historical role, as did the institutionalization of policy principles pursued by these alliances. In comparative terms it is striking that in Scandinavia, universalism seems historically to have emerged as a kind of default option once the alliance between the labor movement and the agrarian parties was established. Equally importantly, universalism, once established as a basic policy principle, had far-reaching and largely unintended consequences in terms of shaping a relatively widespread and uniform notion across class divisions of the political common good.

As the welfare states in Scandinavia expanded, they gained broad support simply because large parts of the populations came to see public services and benefits as attractive, sufficiently so that they were willing to make the sacrifice of accepting that others were gaining even more (Esping-Andersen 1990; Sejersted 2005). Let me at this point add my own perspective on this dynamic to Baldwin's analysis, which is, despite its merits, highly abstract and general. From an anthropological point of view, what matters is not only how people identify with political programs and how they perceive their political interest in the abstract, but what matters to them as they involve themselves in arenas where decisions are made and institutionalized, and how they actually experience being on the receiving end of the welfare state.

What characterized the Scandinavian welfare state model as opposed to other Western models was not only the universalism and the scope of welfare policy as such; the "municipalization" of the welfare state is perhaps equally important. Indeed, Scandinavian political scientists and historians have pointed out that we should rather speak of "the welfare municipality" than "the welfare state" (Baldersheim and Rose 2000; Rose and Ståhlberg 2005). We return to this phenomenon below, but it should be pointed out here that Scandinavian municipalities carry a much larger share of the responsibility for providing the services and benefits that people seem to think of as attractive and important in their daily lives than is the case in other European countries. In Norway, municipalities are mostly very small; the average population size is approximately 5000 (Jensen 2009), and they are multipurpose institutions, covering everything from primary education, major health and welfare services and culture, to a broad range of infrastructural responsibilities. Moreover, they are governed through political representation, the backbone of which are political parties based on mass membership and, as indicated in Chap. 3, a considerable degree of membership-based forms of social control. Elected politicians in Norwegian municipal assemblies, further-more, score on average somewhat lower than the general population on socioeconomic criteria. Their level of education largely mirrors the aver-age among the population (a little over 30% have some form of college education) (Statistics Norway, ssb.no/valg/statistikker/kommvalg).

In democratic societies, representative government is a universal ideal. However, for a variety of reasons, along the chain of representa-tion much of the direct social control that exists in real communities and social networks tends to be lost on the way and substituted by chains of bureaucratic and political command. Two of the major interrelated factors behind this seem to be, first, the deep cleavages resulting from class-based, elitist appropriation of representative functions (Esping-Andersen 2002; Glyn 2006; Heinrich 2010), and second, social relations of dependency between those representing and those being represented (Fukuyama 2014; Minkin 2014). The apt conceptualization of the sec-ond aspect is clientelism, or patrimonialism (Roniger 1998; Collins 2011; Piattoni 2001). Clientelism denotes a social relationship that involves asymmetrical reciprocity, meaning, for example, that a represent-ative (formal or informal) provides his or her clients with resources that are otherwise very hard to get access to, often due to their peripheral position in relation to centers of power (Papakostas 2001). As a result, representatives may utilize their position as intermediaries and brokers, and use it as a means for securing loyalty. In modern democracies, mod-ernist theories tell us, clientelism is no longer "needed" due to the open competition in elections, facilitated by a transparent public sphere. Thus clientelism often serves as a marker of the distinction between "primi-tive" and "modern" political systems, serving, for example, self-righteous perceptions of Southern Europe as less "mature" than proper democ-racies farther north. However unfruitful such an assumption may be, a minimum requirement for any study of representation involves asking what actually prevents representatives from departing from the collective interests of those they represent. There is hardly any doubt that doing exactly this may, at least in many cases, appear attractive.

Consequently, for those represented the problem becomes one of social control within the context of bureaucratic institutions. One solu-tion to this problem may be, as indicated by both Barnes and Baldwin above, cultivating the strength of horizontal ties that include sanction-ing mechanisms which are not only activated by the end of the term, but are morally binding on a daily basis and thus secure commitments to a program. The crucial aspect of this is that the program legitimates the making of claims from the bottom up, claims that representatives cannot ignore without paying a price. At the heart of this, of course, is the legitimacy of any political function or institution established to exercise the collective will in the democratic sense. Basically, it is a matter of controlling the interests of representatives and shaping the conditions according to which they are able to craft their own careers.

THE VIRTUES OF BUREAUCRACY

However, representative government involves much more than just political legitimacy in this rather narrow sense. At stake in all contemporary democracies is not only political representation, but also popular control of the institutions of the state, or the public sector. Since the 1970s and 1980s, Western states have developed and cultivated technical ways of governing the state that has made public institutions and bureaucratic machineries more autonomous vis-à-vis the public and the population at large (Esping-Andersen 2002; Siltala 2013). Sometimes this development is spoken of as "new public management (NPM)," referring to a set of measures that make public institutions more manageable, including market-like mechanisms such as those enabling political and managerial decision makers to order a certain amount and quality of services from those levels directly responsible for delivering them according to a set ratio between capacity/resources and "demand" (Minogue et al. 1998; Christensen and Lægreid 2003). However, in practice it often seems to mean something quite different, perhaps most typically the systematization of managers' ability to make claims on their subordinates without having to negotiate the terms.

Public sector reforms from the 1980s onwards clearly reflect a common tendency in Western states that political elites cannibalize the widespread popular frustration with bureaucratic dominance, insensitivity, and waste (Du Gay 2005). Welfare states that have become overwhelmed by popular demands to which they lack resources to respond, have provided fertile ground for the emergence of political elites arguing for fiscal austerity, efficiency, and modernization. Although arguments for measures that increase institutional control from the top may have some merits, they do not necessarily provide answers to the original problem, which is largely about political promises and the actual capacity to realize them. In the aftermath of World War II, welfare states gained increasing support, and although popular frustration with specific dysfunctions clearly grew in the 1970s and 1980s, this frustration hardly amounted to a unison call for the downscaling of the welfare state as such. But increasingly public sector reforms have made it much harder to make direct claims on the state, as public institutions have become more obsessed with selectivism and conditionality. In a way, this was the intention and the point. Although such reforms most often are promoted as antibureaucratic measures to increase the availability of public services, the major reason for introducing them has been the need to spend fewer resources, reduce demand, and control resources from the top of organizational pyramids. Above all, public employees need to be controlled so as not to be tempted to involve themselves too intensely in the needs of those who require and are entitled to their services (Siltala 2013). This represents a fundamental risk to the integrity of the institution, or its managers, who increasingly depend on their superiors. In the reformed public sector, managers at all levels are becoming more personally dependent on those who order their services. Only rarely, it seems, have they retained the "Weberian" professional integrity that previously enabled them to make claims with reference to ethics, quality, and other aspects pertaining to the mandate given to them through political promises, user rights, service regulations, and the like.

These observations may serve to illustrate that whereas public services previously served as a primary interface between the population and the state, where claims were forwarded, negotiations carried out, and adjustments made, they are increasingly the end of a production line far beyond popular influence and control. This, to my mind, raises the question of how and in which way the state and the public sector represent the popular will, a question that goes way beyond conventional/technical standards of accountability. Can a public bureaucracy serve representative functions? The question emerges from the observation that a major transformation of modern Western states has taken place, one which to some extent has turned the institutions of the welfare state against those they are set to serve. One place to start looking is, as indicated above, at what happens at the interface between the state and the population, or receivers/users of public services. Another is to investigate the identity of bureaucrats and what shapes these identities. As Michael Lipsky demonstrated so vividly in his classic, *Street-Level Bureaucracy* (1980), bureaucrats responsible for balancing resource control with the mandate to embrace the needs of the people they are supposed to assist, tend to live in two worlds simultaneously. They need to be loyal to their bosses, but at the same time try to realize policy intentions and cultivate professional ethics. As all bureaucratic labor involves some sort of discretion, this involves making choices and taking risks. Sometimes street-level bureaucrats (as all other bureaucrats, I would contend) are exposed to situations characterized by a double bind, and they face fundamental dilemmas. In such situations, ethics and loyalty are not the only frames of reference: their understanding of the relative strength of the interests that will sanction their choices are of key importance. In my own ethnographic explorations of local politics and service provision in Norway, I have been interested in precisely this. Political representatives, administrative bosses, and professional service providers all tend to see themselves as caught in a sort of double-bind situation; only the naïve or cynical don't. This is not, on my part, a claim concerning the moral quality of these actors, but a description of a certain subjectivity that tends to develop as an integral part of the political economy of the welfare state. Put crudely, the Norwegian welfare state is very ambitious, and welfare ambitions (which to a large extent have been transformed into individual rights) and policy intentions tend to be interpreted literally. This makes for very strong claims on the part of the population. In the Norwegian contexts, in my view it appears striking that people who do not receive services they are entitled to not only get frustrated, but are also surprised, and start trying to identify the error. The same is often the case with street-level bureaucrats and even their colleagues at higher administrative levels. I have repeatedly observed situations where they realize that their mandate cannot be realized due to lack of resources, and then make more or less desperate attempts to document this to their superiors so that the situation can be mended. This may seem like a naïve approach, but it is surely not, at least not in most cases. Their worlview constitutes an important aspect of what we may call a "climate of claims." The choice of interpreting the utopian policies pursued by state political elites (including all governments of all political colors over the last decades) literally makes a big difference, because of the legitimate pressure it enables various interests to direct against the public sector—and here I do not primarily refer to political representatives, but to the public bureaucracy, municipalities in particular—often resonates with the dilemmas experienced by those who are directly responsible for providing public services.

THE THIRD WAY

Returning now to the question of how public institutions may serve representative functions beyond the purely political chain, we may take a closer look at how institutions that provide the contexts in which people experience "the state" actually work, that is, what types of relationships constitute them and contribute to shaping their encounters with those who need and/or want services. This is what I in part tried to do in Chap. 3. Although the term "bureaucracy" has become burdened with a chain of depressive connotations, for my purposes it is useful to restore its original meaning (in Weber's sense). I take bureaucracy to mean hierarchies of power that, through strict divisions of labor based on delegated authority and professional competence, manage specific common goods according to a combination of defined criteria, procedures, and discretion. In Max Weber's terms, neutrality is a specific bureaucratic prerequisite and ideal, enabling an organizational capacity to deal with individual cases as instances of general categories, strictly separated from the bureaucrats' personal interests and views of those acting on the bureaucratic organization's behalf (Weber 1978, 1994; Du Gay 2005). Professional integrity is of vital importance, as the domain of judgment pertaining to a given type of competence may be challenged both by pressure from the environment (friends, kin, powerful individuals, etc.), but also from within the institution and from above: political decisions may in some cases contradict basic regulations and ethical codes, and bureaucratic superiors seeking better control (or support, legitimacy, or whatever) may undermine basic policy intentions or laws (Papakostas 2001). In many ways, bureaucracies have to be conservative and contribute to preventing misuse of power by impatient power holders, in much the same way as do the courts.

No wonder, then, that public bureaucracies almost never seem to work according to the ideal. As Paul Du Gay has convincingly argued, bureaucratic ideals and more or less well–functioning bureaucracies are essential prerequisites for most of the qualities of democratic societies, and thus it is problematic that so much scholarly critique seems romantically to take as its departure the belief that we can manage without them (Du Gay 2000). The reform programs sweeping the public sector in Western countries since the 1980s have largely been promoted under the banner of freedom. Less bureaucracy supposedly increases individual freedom, and techniques of governance (steering by objectives, outsourcing, audit technology, etc.) are supposed to make public bureaucracies more transparent and more sensitive to people's real needs. It is interesting to note that such essentially romantic visions concerning the role of bureaucracy in modern society resonates so well with both the conservative–liberal critique of the welfare state and the social democratic attempts (from the 1990s onward) to develop a new social contract along the lines of the philosophy of the "Third Way." Anthony Giddens, in the capacity of serving as a major intellectual inspiration in the Third Way movement, has formulated his vision in a way that I find highly illustrative. In their book *The New Egalitarianism* (Giddens and Diamond 2005) Anthony Giddens and Patrick Diamond (special advisor to Tony Blair) present a "third way," a recipe for a more egalitarian order. Here they place welfare policies of the kind pursued in Scandinavia in the category of "old egalitarianism," arguing that it is doomed to fail because it "was inclined to treat rights and unconditional claims" (p. 107). Continues by stating that

> New egalitarianism ties rights to corresponding responsibilities. The new egalitarianism thus introduces two elements of conditionality into the means-tested welfare system. Benefits depend not only on a person's needs but also on his or her behavior. (Giddens and Diamond 2005: 107)

Giddens and Diamond's perspective on what may be the problem with public responsibility/state policy, too little conditionality, is illustrative of a distinctive perspective on egalitarianism, but also of the nature of bureaucracy in welfare states. Insofar as they view "unconditional claims" as something that influences the morale of the marginalized in negative ways, they assume that people seeking public assistance are in need of people (elites) and institutions capable of setting, or dictating such conditions. Giddens and Diamond do not reflect more about this, and thus it seems safe to assume that they feel intellectually and socially at home in such a position. This I find fascinating. This position is a distinctly elitist one, and as such, it is "beyond left and right," as Giddens himself has (nonironically) phrased it. Assuming the responsibility to manipulate the conditions for other people's access seems to feel very natural from such a perspective.

As one of the intellectual inspirations for the Third Way approach that achieved status as the common denominator for European Social Democratic parties in the 1990s, originally manifesting itself in Tony

Blair's rise to power in the British Labour Party and, in 1996, the British government, Anthony Giddens was an important part of a greater wave of change. His vision to cultivate a new sense of morality among the marginalized under the guidance of the guardians of conditionality reflects itself in what British historian Lewis Minkin has called *The Blair Supremacy* (Minkin 2014). Many of the same reform ideas guided both welfare policy and Labour's party management. In much the same way as Giddens sees "the old egalitarianism" as a dysfunctional system that leaves too much leeway for people in need of public support to undermine their own interests (read: morality), Tony Blair viewed the Labour Party's organizational framework as dysfunctional for realizing his vision. According to Minkin, "The past multilayered loyalty of the party machine to the party, the movement and the leader was not turned into a [repoliticised] loyalty to the Leader" (Minkin 2014: 664). The party's collective leadership's role was swiftly transformed from one of securing democratic anchorage for the party's program into one of defending the leader. The overarching vision was to substitute its degenerate character with a modernizing revolution in Britain. The party largely became a set of audiences to be moved by the leader, expected to serve as guarantor for the production of good results for Blair. Labour was to move away from "obsessive processology" and thus able to concentrate on "what will deliver for Tony" (ibid., 666). At a later stage Blair's increasing discomfort with bureaucratic routines inspired him to go more directly after "unfiltered, uncontrolled party activity" because he saw it as representing a threat to the government and the people (ibid., 680).

Maybe Minkin is exaggerating. Clearly, his sympathies are with the "traditional" grassroots of the Labour Party. Yet regardless of Tony Blair's motivation, the general trend seems well documented and is wholly in harmony with what the concept "modernization" has come to mean in terms of democratic governance in Britain and elsewhere. In 2003, the new Norwegian government renamed the Ministry of Regional and Municipal Affairs, "The Ministry of Municipal Affairs and Modernization," immediately launching a program for municipal amalgamation on the basis of the idea that bigger and more centralized municipalities will be more democratic and efficient. In line with this, the government has also implemented administrative reforms and control techniques inspired by New Public Management, ideas on a grand scale. The felt need to "modernize" bureaucratic organizations and institutions is clearly not a purely neoliberal agenda, but a much more general trend that concerns the distribution of power in democratic societies, access to and influence over public institutions in particular. It is not very hard to understand that the strategy pursued by Tony Blair reflects a profound dilemma among political and managerial elites in democratic countries. A major obstacle to political and managerial success for such elites is lack of autonomy (Sennett 1993; Fukuyama 2011). In most situations the barrier they encounter in their quest for autonomy—the ability to realize their programs—is the resources consumed by big public institutions and the rules and procedures blocking initiatives from those who are supposed to control these institutions. As bureaucracies grow according to the increasing responsibility resulting from political initiatives they are set to implement, bureaucracies tend, as Weber pointed out, to develop a certain conservatism. Existing responsibilities have to be aligned with new ones, and in order to do that bureaucracies have to be concerned with both continuity and consistency. Without some autonomy, this becomes impossible. The relative autonomy of any bureaucracy rests heavily on its ability to cultivate integrity and, in the last instance, the right not to follow political orders if such orders undermine already existing responsibilities. Both political and managerial elites may have many reasons to challenge this autonomy, as their political and personal success depends upon getting access to the massive resources controlled by public institutions.

Tony Blair's reorganization of the British Labour Party may illuminate how this dynamic is socially organized. It is interesting to note that both romantic, antibureaucratic critique, on the one hand, and contemporary managerialism and political modernization visions are in fact based on the same notion that bureaucracies are supposed to be hierarchical machines, and serving as tools for those in the position to give orders. The difference is that in the romantic visions this is seen as a threat to our humanity, and in the other it is viewed as an ideal. Both versions are clearly erroneous in the sense that bureaucracies are not, and were never meant to be, purely hierarchical chains of command. They are also, as noted above, conservative guarantees that make it possible to limit the potential damage done by the whims of politics or impatient leadership. The mooring needed for the relative autonomy they require in order to be able to cultivate it is to be found in specific types of social relations. Professional integrity and horizontal solidarity (shared understanding on the part of professional collectives) are, in functional terms, necessary because political whims and impatient leadership may otherwise appropriate and abuse it. What Blair did, according to Lewis Minkin, was to make the Labour Party leadership (and, ultimately the party members) dependent on him. His success in terms of political delivery substituted consensus, the majority vote, and conventional chains of representation as the paramount mechanisms for internal loyalty and public support.

Historically, personal loyalty has been a major building block in the establishment of political power in most societies. In "primitive" tribal societies where kinship is the major organizing principle, personal loyalty tends to follow the patrilineal principle and extensions thereof, as in the case of "predatory kinship" (Searle 1988; in Collins 2011). In the feudal context, it was based on a combination of kinship, categorical rank, and territoriality. In the Roman world, personal loyalty was a basic ingredient of the protodemocratic public, of electoral support for individual politicians, as well as of bureaucratic functions (Mouritsen 2001; Nicols 2013). In anthropological studies of Europe, the notion of "patron–client relations" or, more simply "clientelism," constitutes the standard conceptualization of the mixing of personal loyalty with more complex institutional systems in which other competing forms of loyalty were simultaneously cultivated (Pitt-Rivers 1954; Wolf 1966). As indicated above, clientelism is normally seen as a personal relation between a socially superior individual who, by virtue of his resources and contacts, is able to offer an inferior person protection in exchange for loyal support. Of course, the latter becomes dependent on the former and the relationship is one of asymmetry. It seems clear that a major part of what goes under the name of "modernization" in political and managerial discourses in institutional governance is precisely about reintroducing or reinforcing relations of personal dependency; I guess "neoclientelism" may serve as a precise conceptualization of this phenomenon (Siltala 2013). In modern bureaucracies, however, as well as in the Blair case, personal loyalty is not simply a relationship of almost complete dependency; one in which the client's only possibility for voicing protest is to choose to subordinate himself to another patron. It is a more subtle relationship in which the subordinate person, say a chief bureaucrat, may have a considerable degree of autonomy, both in terms of the right to negotiate (some of) the conditions of obedience and in terms of exit (quitting the job or asking to be transferred). Yet, in "modernized" policy worlds, any bureaucratic manager is personally dependent on her superior in the sense that the only alternative to following orders is to "choose" to resign. Even in cases where professional ethics would call for serious objections to a given policy implementation measure, for example, on the ground that it may threaten the quality of service for all or some recipients (and quality reduction is not a part of the policy), loyalty to the organization is paramount. In this way, it may become very hard to prevent bureaucratic public institutions from going down the path of politicization. Devoid of any robust social mechanisms allowing for some institutional backing of those responsibilities that at the moment may seem less important for politicians who want to deliver fast, managers may become like the Labour Party leadership, people whose futures depend on the strength of their active contribution to the common good, which in this context comes to mean that which may be realized as a result of Blair's success.

By focusing on the social relations upon which bureaucratic functions are based, instead of on abstract idealized models of how proper bureaucracies are supposed to work, or romantic criticism of the necessary evils of bureaucracy as such, I hope to have indicated that the analytical modeling of any really existing bureaucracy needs to take into account how organizational power is distributed between different sets of actors, and how these actors relate to each other. In the Norwegian case, this may be particularly fruitful, I argue, because the welfare state depends very heavily on bureaucratic functions. The bureaucratic management of extremely ambitious welfare policies has not to any great extent given rise to a popular feeling of being alienated by bureaucratic dominance. This is surprising and needs an explanation.

In *The New Egalitarianism* Giddens and Diamond do not speak of bureaucracy as such, but as my discussion above indicates, my major concern in this section is precisely the specific combination of welfare state visions and policies on the one hand, and the bureaucratic organization of the great responsibility they entail. Giddens and Diamond's perspective reveals, to my mind at least, that the very widespread belief that "new egalitarianism" (which in their terms, I suppose, means greater equality and more justice) depends on more targeted welfare services. Better targeting is needed for two main reasons: the public acceptance of welfare spending rests on the bureaucracy's ability to prevent misuse; and targeting makes it possible to establish a moral contract (conditionality) that transforms welfare services/benefits into something positive. It builds character and promotes individual careers. This way of thinking is not a peripheral aspect of the Third Way movement, undoubtedly, the most widely supported social democratic movement in the world since the neoliberal turn in the early 1980s. As such, it is indicative of one of my main points: the widespread frustration with bureaucratic dysfunctions and failed welfare state ambitions can be easily explained by reference to Giddens and Diamond's recipe. Such problems are not necessarily an effect of the nature of (growing) bureaucracies, but perhaps mainly a product of how bureaucracies may break bad when brought under the influence of romantic policy makers. It seems reasonable to say, some 20 years after Tony Blair took over government in Britain, that such romantics have carried out the same job as liberals do when they use the same type of romanticism as a rhetoric device to dismantle the welfare state project altogether.

Towards a New State?

One of Anthony Gidden's intellectual ancestors, Richard Titmuss, was a major inspiration behind the Beveridge Plan and its realization in Britain in the early post-World War II period. He argued that welfare policy, in order to have real redistributive effects, build trust, and inspire a sense among the population of having shared interests, has to be based on the principle of universalism (Titmuss 1968; in Pierson and Castles 2000). By universalism, Titmuss referred to welfare benefits and services that are more or less automatically available to anyone who meets certain broadly defined criteria. In theory this logic transforms much of the hierarchy-driving dynamic entailed by conditionality, because welfare benefits and services become largely needs driven rather than based upon complex discretionary processes. Although the bureaucratic system established to implement universalism may be both large and complex, universalism may be very easy to handle, and thus both cheap and efficient. We may add, also, that universalism carries the potential for establishing nonhumiliating encounters with public bureaucracies. As long as bureaucrats are not primarily interested in testing whether you qualify, but professionally devoted to assisting you in getting what you need, interests are shared and power differentials may be minimized. Referring to the early post-World War II British welfare state, Titmuss pointed out that

> Slowly and painfully the lesson was learnt that if such services were to be utilized in time and were to be effective in action in a highly differentiated, unequal and class-saturated society, they had to be delivered through

socially approved channels; that is to say without loss of self-respect by the users and their families. (Titmuss in Pierson and Castles 2000: 43)

Titmuss' idea of universalism has been treated here as an ideal type. Although at first glance it may seem wildly unrealistic as the point of departure for policy making, it is important to point out that the ideal type is not as far removed from practical realities as it may seem. Giddens' portrayal of "old egalitarianism" represents one version of the common theme that there is no alternative to the Third Way, everything else is either "old" (and thus, in Giddens' view past and irrelevant) or neoliberal. Despite the fact that the welfare state in Titmuss' vision was a reference point for the European Union up to the financial crisis in 2007, today its relevance has been radically reduced by the combined effect of widespread resignation and the unprecedented acceleration of inequality in the West (Glyn 2006). One of the more recent, and harshest, critics of bureaucracy, anthropologist and anarchist David Graeber, expresses this in the following way:

> The European social welfare state, with its free education and universal health care, can justly be considered – as Pierre Bourdieu once remarked – one of the greatest achievements of human civilization. But at the same time, in taking forms of willful blindness typical of the powerful and giving them the prestige of science – for instance, by adopting a whole series of assumptions about the meaning of work, family, neighborhood, knowledge, health, happiness, or success that had almost nothing to do with the way poor or working-class people actually lived their lives, let alone what they found meaningful in them – it set itself up for a fall. And fall it did. It was precisely the uneasiness this blindness created even in the minds of its greatest beneficiaries that allowed the Right to mobilize popular support for the policies that have gutted and devastated even the most successful of these programs since the eighties. And how was this uneasiness expressed? Largely, by the feeling that bureaucratic authority, by its very nature, represented a kind of war against the human imagination. (Graeber 2015: 82)

Graeber's diagnosis resonates well with many other scholarly, political, and more popular criticisms and frustrations, including the fear that started to grow in the 1970s that the Scandinavian welfare state, the Swedish in particular, were about to turn into bureaucratic monsters (Graubard 1986). However, the diagnosis is plainly off the mark in several respects. Most important perhaps, in Scandinavia, where the welfare state has definitely not (yet) fallen, is people's trust in the state and its bureaucracy is still quite strong (Rothstein 2011). The desire to develop more and better welfare services and benefits is perhaps the only thing that unites them politically. In much the same way as Giddens, Graeber thinks that the tragedy of the Left is that it never realized that the natural evils of bureaucracy undermine the welfare state as political project. One alternative hypothesis, and a more reasonable one, I would argue, is that it is not necessarily the natural evils of bureaucracy that drives people away from the social democratic welfare state program, but rather the gradual undermining of universalism, which has transformed the public sector in fundamental ways and introduced the logic implicated by Giddens. The ideology of the Third Way, as formulated by Giddens in scholarly terms, is, among other things, a reflection of an elitist desire to make stronger claims on those whose social background, cultural capital, and life trajectories differ from their own. In addition, it is a recipe for constructing bureaucracies that tend to become overwhelmed by unmanageable complexity and at the same time produce widespread humiliation.

Bruce Kapferer and Bjørn Enge Bertelsen have recently argued that contemporary global changes tend to affect the nation state in such a way that it assumes a more "corporate" and "oligarchic" form (Kapferer and Bethelsen 2009: 15). Representative government transmutes into a more managerial form and is increasingly driven by ambitions similar to those characterizing business corporations. In the Scandinavian welfare states, such transformations may be less dramatic than in Britain and the United States, for example, but nevertheless clearly evident from waves of privatization, massive liberalization of the labor market, and the reorganization of public institutions into a hierarchical ordering of executing units, respectively. Policy goals such as social investment and social integration are evaluated primarily according to whether they pay off, the power (and salaries) of managers is increased at the cost of street-level bureaucracies, and austerity measures are prioritized to the extent that the consequences of capacity problems—reduced quality of public services and increasing means testing—no longer influence decision making to any significant extent.

State orders, Kapferer and Bertelsen argue,

> are being reconfigured after the ideals of contemporary business and industrial corporations. Thus, there is a move away from the impersonal rationalist, equalizing, bureaucratic schemes that dominated ruling governing

institutions of nation-states to managerial, person-centered, even autocratic and hierarchical orders, that espouses ideologies of flexibility, individual-responsible or accountable decision-making, and transparency.

...[T]he corporate state form is an abandonment of the social project of the nation-state – that is, the concern to meet the crisis of power at the center of the state by commanding the institutions for the reproduction of the social. (Kapferer and Bertelsen 2009: 15)

In this perspective, public bureaucracy in the classic form is seen as "equalizing" and an institutional guarantee for "the social project of the nation state." This clearly breaks with the romantic agenda underlying much of the criticism of public bureaucracy (Bauman 1989; Sennett 2003; Graeber 2015), and is in line with Du Gay's well-known argument in *In Praise of Bureaucracy* (2003), which is seen by many as a "return to Weber."

In a more down to earth manner, Danish sociologist Kaspersen in his discussion of labor market policy in Norden over the last decades points out that the supposed merits of increasing conditionality lack empirical support. One main reason, he suggests, is the following.

My claim is that we tend to neglect that the state has its own agenda – to remain independent and sovereign – which is always there notwithstanding the political ideologies dominating the current debate in the country among parties and groups. At crucial moments mostly when new external conditions of existence [emerge] this rationality tends to override any other agendas brought forward by the political parties. Any state must struggle for survival as a state and thus many welfare aspects must also be viewed in this light. (Kaspersen 2005: 70)

I find Kaspersen's comment highly relevant and reasonable, and here I repeat my main point: "the state," or rather the different institutions that are supposed to perform the functions attributed to what we call "the state," indeed tend to develop their own agenda, and perhaps the only thing that may prevent these institutions from becoming autonomous, is to retain the mechanisms that allow for some control from below. As noted above, in the aftermath of the financial crisis it has become appallingly clear that European states have followed the path of economic restructuring according to the conventional orthodoxy of EU policy, as the case of Greece most dramatically shows.

In Scandinavia, the Swedish, Danish, and Norwegian states have since the 1990s been profoundly shaped by the felt need to introduce measures to make public institutions controllable from the top (Sejersted 2005; Lindvall and Rothstein 2006; Vohnsen 2013). This involves a combination of austerity measures that have reduced the scope of public services in some areas, and restructured the public sector according to NPM standards, the latter prioritizing a centralization of economic control and decentralization of service providing responsibility within fixed budgets. Accordingly, the line of reasoning in this book takes as its point of departure the assumption that public policy is shaped by power relationships and their dynamic. State elites, broadly speaking, compete over a variety of things, but in Scandinavia the competition for votes seems unusually strongly tied to more and better welfare services. Welfare policies have become a major source of popular concern, and all political parties need to respond to it. However, as resources are scarce, they all focus on how to get value for money, which in practice means trying to find ways to make the public sector more "efficient."

Politically, this strategy seems far more attractive than cutting down on service provision, and thus it constitutes a major interest. The upper layers of the public bureaucracy are directly dependent upon these elites, therefore they tend to identify with the ambition and to realize it through controlling and disciplining the service-providing, lower levels of the public bureaucracy, the municipalities in particular. As a result, a strong tension tends to develop between two opposing interests: the ambition to interpret and deal with the grand ambitions in welfare policy in literal terms, and to limit expenditures. On the face of it, it may seem as if everyone wants both. However, in reality both interests are distributed in complex ways, and empirically it is often difficult to detect where the tension between them actually manifests itself. In practical terms this may seem to boil down to a very simple logic: given the fact that welfare policy is a major source for political support and legitimacy, elites try to have their cake and eat it, too. The dilemma generated by the combination of increasingly ambitious welfare policies (which increasingly are materialized in the form of state-guaranteed individual rights) on the one hand, and the need to cut costs can be decentralized to the municipalities and the service providers. At this level the tension manifests itself in a different form. Here, local elites, political and administrative, tend to prioritize cost control. A strange gang challenges them, however. This gang includes not only all those who, in times of austerity measures, feel that their rights are threatened, but also many service providers, political representatives who identify with both of these groups, as well as the central state. Political elites in the central state naturally make attempts to craft a direct alliance with users against the service providers and the municipalities, obviously in order to discipline the latter.

One important consequence is that it becomes almost impossible to identify where the accumulated overwhelming responsibility stops being seen as political and becomes administrative and professional (i.e., a collective or personal responsibility of service providers). My point is this: the tension described here mobilized "policy alliances" (Lo 2015) of various kinds, and such alliances may have a significant role to play in challenging elite interests, particularly related to making the service-providing tiers assume responsibility for providing more and better services for less money. The formation of such alliances takes place both within and outside the boundaries of the state, but primarily across them.

The influential historical sociologist Charles Tilly (2005) has formulated the relationship between alliance formation and "state rule" in similar, although much wider terms. He labels the former "trust networks." Tilly emphasizes that the varied forms in which state regimes react to the mobilization of "trust networks" may heavily influence processes of democratization. The trust networks he discusses are of many different types, but he seems mainly to concentrate on those networks that tend to emerge as markets expand. A main problem, he argues, is that "regimes and trust networks often depend on the same resources— labor power, money, information, loyalty, and more" (Tilly 2005: 23). For this reason, such networks are vulnerable to destruction owing to rulers' temptation to seize these resources. But a few processes may promote accommodations and connect trust networks with public politics, thereby establishing some form of mutual, although sometimes highly conflictual, dependency. The present book is partly about how trust networks become integrated into public politics. I look at processes that have promoted such accommodations. In Norway and Scandinavia at large, this seems to have happened to a rather large extent, and I explore some aspects of how this occurred, and why, and examine some of the implications. In comparative terms, popular political mobilization in Scandinavia was quite successful in influencing the state, not only by forcing it to make concessions, but also by integrating forms of trust, horizontal loyalty, and certain values and interests that became important for developing policy, such as individual autonomy and universalism (Vike 2012, 2015). A key issue here, as I understand it, is that under some circumstances trust networks may be able to retain and protect vital resources independently of state power.

References

Arter, David. 2008. *Scandinavian Politics Today*. Manchester: Manchester University Press.

Baldersheim, Harald and Lawrence Rose. 2000. *Det kommunale laboratorium. Teoretiske perspektiver på lokal politikk og organisering*. Bergen: Fagbokforlaget.

Baldwin, Peter. 1990. *The Politics of Social Solidarity Class Bases of the European Welfare State 1875-1975*. Cambridge: Cambridge University Press.

Barnes, J. 1954. Class and Committees in a Norwegian Island Parish. *Human Relations* 7 (1): 39–58.

Barth, Erling et al. 2015: Political Reinforcement: How Rising Inequality Curbs Manifested Welfare Generosity. In *American Political Science* 59 (3): 565–577.

Bauman, Zygmunt. 1989. *Modernity and the Holocaust*. Cambridge: Polity Press.

Christensen, Tom, and Per Lægreid. 2003. *New Public Management: The Transformation of Ideas and Practice*. Hampshire: Ashgate Publishing Limited.

Collins, Randall. 2011. Patrimonial Alliances and Failures of State Penetration: A Historical Dynamic of Crime. Corruption, Gangs, and Mafias. *The Annals of the American Academy of Political and Social Sciences* 636, June: 16–31.

Du Gay, Paul. 2000. *In Praise of Bureaucracy Weber, Organization, Ethics*. London: Sage.

Du Gay, Paul. 2005. *The Values of Bureaucracy*. Oxford/New York: Oxford University Press.

Esping-Andersen, Gösta. 1990. *The Three Worlds of Welfare Capitalism*. Cambridge: Polity Press.

Fukuyama, F. 2011. *The Origin of Political Order From Prehuman Times to the French Revolution*. New York: Farrar, Strauss and Giroux.

Fukuyama, Francis. 2014. *Political Order and Political Decay from the Industrial Revolution to the Globalisation of Democracy*. London: Profile Books.

Giddens, Anthony, and Diamond, Patrick. 2005. The New Egalitarianism: Economic Equality in the UK. In *The New Egalitarianism*, ed. Anthony Giddens and Patrick Diamond. Cambridge: Polity Press.

Graeber, David. 2015. *The Utopia of Rules. On Technology, Stupidity, and the Secret Joys of Bureaucracy*. Brooklyn: Melville House.

Graubard, Stephen R. (ed.). 1986. *Norden: The Passion for Equality*. Oslo: Norwegian University Press.

Glyn, Andrew. 2006. *Capitalism Unleashed. Finance, Globalization, and Welfare.* New York. Oxford University Press.

Higley, John, and Heinrich Best. 2010. *Democratic Elitism: New Theoretical and Comparative Perspectives.* Leiden: Brill Academic Publishers.

Jensen, Bjarne. 2009. *Norske kommuner i et europeisk perspektiv: fakta om struktur.* Rena: Høgskolen i Hedmark.

Kaspersen, Lars Bo. 2005. The Origin, Development, Consolidation and Transformation of the Danish Welfare State. In *The Normative Foundations of the Welfare State. The Nordic Experience*, eds. Kuhnle, Stein, and Kildal, Nanna, 52–73. New York: Routledge.

Kapferer, Bruce, and Bertelsen, Bjørn E. 2009. Introduction: The Crisis of Power and Reformations of the State in Globalizing Realities. In *Crisis of the State. War and Social Upheaval*, ed. Bruce Kapferer and Bjørn E Bertelsen. New York: Berghahn Books.

Lindvall, Johannes, and Rothstein, Bo. 2006. Sweden: The Fall of the Strong State. *Scandinavian Political Studies* 29 (1): 47–63.

Lipsky, Michael. 1980. *Street-Level Bureaucracy Dilemmas of the Individual in Public Services.* New York: Russel Sage Foundation.

Lo, Christian. 2015. *How to Win Friends and Influence Policy: An Ethnographic Study of Government and Governance in Municipal Policy Development.* Phd. Thesis, Bodø: Nord universitet.

Minkin, Lewis. 2014. *The Blair Supremacy a Study in the Politics of Labour's Party Management.* Manchester: Manchester University Press.

Minogue, Martin, Charles Polidano, and David Hulme (eds.). 1998. *Beyond the New Public Management Changing Ideas and Practices in Governance.* Cheltenham: Edward Elgar.

Mouritsen, Henrik. 2001. *Plebs and Politics in the Late Roman Republic.* Leiden: Cambridge University Press.

Nicols, John. 2013. *Civic Patronage in the Roman Empire.* Leiden: Brill.

Papakostas, Apostolis 2001. Why is there no Clientelism in Sweden? In *Clientelism, Interests, and Democratic Representatio. the European Experience in Historical and Comparative Perspective*, ed. Simona Piattoni, 31–54. Cambridge: Cambridge University Press.

Piattoni, Simona (ed.). 2001. *Clientelism, Interests, and Democratic Representation the European Experience in Historical and Comparative Perspective.* Cambridge: Cambridge University Press.

Pitt-Rivers, Julian. 1954. *The People of the Sierra.* Chicago: University of Chicago Press.

Roniger, Luis. 1998. Civil Society, Patronage, and Democracy. In *Real Civil Societies. Dilemmas of Institutionalization*, ed. Jeffrey Alexander, 66–84. London: Sage.

Rose, Lawrence E., and Ståhlberg, Krister. 2005. The Nordic Countries: Still the Promised Land. In *Comparing Local Governance Trends and Developments*, ed. Bas Denters and Lawrence Rose. New York: Houndsmills.

Rothstein, Bo. 2011. *The Quality of Government Corruption, Social Trust, and Inequality in International Perspective*. Chicago: University of Chicago Press.

Searle, Eleanor. 1988. *Predatory Kinship and the Creation of Norman Power. 840–1066*. Berkeley and Los Angeles: University of California Press.

Sejersted, Francis. 2005. *Sosialdemokratiets tidsalder: Norge og Sverige i det 20. århundre*. Oslo: Pax.

Sennett, Richard 1993. *Authority*. London: Faber & Faber.

Sennett, Richard. 2003. *Respect in a World of Inequality*. New York: W.W. Norton & Company.

Sørensen, Øystein, and Bo Stråth. 1997. *The Cultural Construction of Norden*. Oslo: Scandinavian University Press.

Stenius, Henrik. 2010. Nordic Associational Life in a European and an Inter-Nordic Perspective. In *Nordic Associations in a European Perspective*, ed. Henrik Stenius and Risto Alapuro. Baden-Baden: Nomos.

Siltala, Juha 2013. New Public Management: The Evidence-Based Worst Practice? *Administration & Society* 45 (4): 468–493.

Tilly, Charles. 2005. *Trust and Rule*. Cambridge: Cambridge University Press.

Titmuss, Richard. 1968. *Commitment to Welfare*. London: Allen and Unwin.

Titmuss, Richard. 2000. Universalism Versus Selection. In *The Welfare State Reader*, ed. Christopher Pierson and Francis G Castles, 42–51. Cambridge: Polity Press.

Vike, Halvard. 2012. Varianter av vest-europeiske statsformasjoner–Utkast til en historisk antropologi. *Norsk antropologisk tidsskrift* 23 (2): 126–142.

Vike, H. 2015. Likhetens natur. *Norsk antropologisk tidsskrift* 25 (1): 7–21.

Weber, Max. 1978. *Economy and Society: An Outline of Interpretive Sociology*. Los Angeles: University of California Press.

Weber, Max. 1994. *Weber: Political Writings*. Cambridge: Cambridge University Press.

Wolf, Eric. 1966. Kinship, Friendship, and Patron-Client Relations in Complex Societies. In *The Social Anthropology of Complex Societies*, ed. Michael Banton, 1–23.

CHAPTER 5

The Politics of Resistance

INTRODUCTION

Francis Fukuyama, in a little section of his influential work, *Origins of Political Order*, pays a visit to Denmark (Fukuyama 2011: 431–434). In this section, which is entitled, "Getting to Denmark," Fukuyama reflects on what he regards as modern Scandinavia's extraordinary historical trajectory. He identifies the particular dynamic that generated relatively peaceful transitions from a feudal-like social order to democratic welfare capitalism. According to Fukuyama, Denmark's transformations are above all characterized by the combination of a strong state (which from a very early stage secured some *rechtstaat* structures that, among other things, facilitated the development of a vibrant capitalist agricultural economy) and popular mobilization leading to a type of gradual democratic development. In Denmark, popular political mobilization did not trigger major violent reactions from the old elites, even much less so, in fact, than was the case in Britain, which is the prototypical European case of a nonrevolutionary path to constitutional democracy. Concerning "how to get to Denmark," Fukuyama writes:

> Political liberty – that is, the ability of societies to rule themselves – does not depend only on the degree to which a society can mobilize opposition to centralized power and impose constitutional constraints on the state. It must also have a state that is strong enough to act when action is required. (Ibid.: 431)

© The Author(s) 2018
H. Vike, *Politics and Bureaucracy in the Norwegian Welfare State*,
Approaches to Social Inequality and Difference,
https://doi.org/10.1007/978-3-319-64137-9_5

Denmark did indeed have a strong state. However, by the year 1500, Fukuyama points out, it was not at all obvious that the nature of change in Denmark or the rest of Scandinavia would differ from that of any other early modern state-organized society in early modern Europe. But the effects of the Protestant Reformation were tremendous, particularly in terms of the path it paved for the spread of literacy among the peasantry. Peasant enlightenment generated a new sense of individuality, as well as political mobilization and economic modernization. In contrast to Britain, representative democracy in Denmark emerged not from a feudal institution, Parliament, but from a more or less continuous struggle from below to increase citizens' rights. Danish peasants (who during the mid-1800s transformed themselves into commercially oriented farmers) were not alone in this struggle: constitutional democracy emerged from a broad alliance across the major class divisions, as both national liberals and the rising labor movement joined in. The old elites were deeply divided: the king had managed to marginalize the class of large landowners and establish a form of absolute rule, but became increasingly dependent on the urban bourgeoisie as well as the peasant farmers (as taxpayers, soldiers, and economic modernizers; Knudsen and Rothstein 1994; Østergård 1992).

A number of other factors were involved in this historical trajectory. Fukuyama concludes that the Danish case is "full of historical accidents and contingent circumstances," and adds that these "cannot be duplicated elsewhere" (2011: 434). Nevertheless, he points out that there appear to be many different ways to "get to Denmark" as long as there is some combination of a strong state, rule of law, accountable government, and organized opposition from "below." As noted in the previous chapter, Charles Tilly (2005), in a comparatively oriented study, has emphasized that the varied forms in which state regimes react to the mobilization of "trust networks" may heavily influence processes of democratization. The trust networks he discusses are of many different types, but he seems mainly to concentrate on those networks that tend to emerge as markets expand. A main problem, he argues, is that "regimes and trust networks often depend on the same resources—labor power, money, information, loyalty, and more" (Tilly 2005: 23). For this reason, such networks are vulnerable to destruction owing to rulers' temptation to seize these resources. Nevertheless, a few processes may promote accommodations and connect trust networks with public politics, thereby establishing some form of mutual—although sometimes highly conflictual—dependency.

"Getting to Denmark" is partly about how trust networks may become integrated into public politics, and in this chapter, I look at processes that have promoted such accommodations. In Scandinavia, this seems to have happened to a rather large extent, and here I explore some aspects of how this occurred, and why, and examine some of the implications. In comparative terms, popular political mobilization in Scandinavia was quite successful in influencing the state, not only by forcing it to make concessions, but also by integrating forms of trust, horizontal loyalty, and certain values and interests that became important for developing policy, such as individual autonomy and universalism (Vike 2012, 2015). A key issue here, as I understand it, is that under some circumstances trust networks may be able to retain and protect vital resources independently of state power.

The present chapter provides a historical review of some important instances of political challenges to state power from below. In addition, it includes an attempt to sketch some important phases in state building and state institutions in Denmark/Norway leading up to the present. Through the latter part of the chapter, I substantiate my claim that municipal politics in Norway have generally been heavily influenced by organized interests (trust networks) which to some extent have been able to challenge the logics of state governance, and assume that the relative success of such challenges may in part explain the emergence of the welfare state as we know it. In Norway in particular, local institutions, municipalities, above all, have been key arenas for the social organization of political interests, and have only partially served as extensions of state power. Local political institutions are highly "porous" and allow political interests to operate both within and beyond the formal boundaries of "the state" (represented by the municipality) and the interests of elites who guard those boundaries and the political–bureaucratic organization these elites are supposed to protect. This phenomenon, it seems to me, has some interesting historical roots, which I explore in some detail in the first part of this chapter. In Norway, and in Scandinavia at large, "grassroots" political mobilization appears historically to have been strong enough to dispute state power in serious ways, but yet at the same time it was not normally seen as deeply threatening (Skirbekk 2010). Grassroots mobilizations were rarely crushed, and were able to evolve in the form of trust networks that were extended from the local level over time. They did not simply become absorbed by the hierarchical, and partly clientelistic, logic of the state apparatus (Piattoni 2001).

As Bo Stråth has pointed out, the seemingly common view that the Scandinavian welfare state model arose from some general, traditional, and widespread will to agree, a culture of consensus, "is not very relevant when considering Scandinavian political culture" (Stråth 2005: 41). In historical terms there seems to be little evidence to support the assumption that a "passion for equality" (Graubard 1986) has permeated "Scandinavian culture." Until quite recently, particularly so in Norway and Denmark (somewhat less so in Sweden), processes of change were characterized principally by intense conflict. In my perspective, "equality" is more an outcome of such conflicts than an overarching value related to "a culture of consensus." Thus, what interests me in this context is the form and dynamic of such conflicts, as well as the institutional features emerging from them. It seems to me that the Scandinavian states went a long way towards incorporating (some of) the tensions that contributed to forming them, and institutionalized these conflicts by attempting to domesticate interests that opposed state policies. In this sense, egalitarianism can be seen as, among other things, a structural *and* cultural aspect of a specific institutional dynamic: institutionalized resistance, if you will. I use the expression "institutionalized resistance" heuristically in order to pinpoint ways in which conflicting interests are played out not only outside, but also within the state as more or less normal routine. In the first main section, I investigate the forms of political opposition that began to occur in the first phase of political modernization in the late seventeenth century and continued into the twentieth, and discuss some aspects of their form and their effects. First, however, I discuss the nature of political interests that developed among the Norwegian "peasantry" prior to and during this period.

OF PEASANTS AND STATE CAPITALISM

In the introduction to this volume (Chap. 1), it was noted that John Barnes' anthropological construction of the island parish of Bremnes involved the observation that "part-time peasants" took part in an egalitarian political order of a transitional kind (Barnes 1954). Barnes emphasized its transnationality because he assumed that what he regarded as a power vacuum was probably in the process of being filled by a more active, modern state formation, and because the class system was expanding. To some extent, he may have been right, but his observations seem to lend themselves to a different interpretation.

What he observed (or failed to observe) may not have been so much a vacuum as an expression of the way in which the Danish, and later the Swedish and Norwegian, state actually worked in places like Bremnes. When Fukuyama speaks of "strong states" as one important condition in the formation of democratic societies, he is somewhat imprecise. In Scandinavia, it was perhaps not the strength of the state that was the salient feature historically, but rather its peculiar unitary nature and its ability to adapt to (and gradually transform) local realities and networks. As Henrik Stenius (2010), Tim Knudsen (2000), and many others have pointed out, the Reformation put an end to subcultural plural- ism in a seemingly radical way. This was achieved, it should be noted, not through the elimination of subcultures as such, but rather by sub- suming them all under one, singular, and conformist authority in reli- gious, administrative, and political terms. In this way, the church, the educational system, the local courts, and municipal institutions could do much of the work of the state, that is, perform some kind of "indirect rule" (Tilly 1990).

In this case, the mediating factor was not primarily powerful interme- diaries but rather institutions that had emerged partly independently of state power, and partly under local control. This made it relatively easy for the state to exercise its authority through a variety of channels and reach the individual citizen, even his or her inner life, at minimum cost and without having to rely on repressive measures (Knudsen 2000) to any great extent. The mutual social control involved in such alliances provided ample possibilities for enforcing discipline, but not without a price. Social control made state authority relatively sensitive to influ- ence from below, inasmuch as the institutions upon which state authority rested were partly external to it and were dominated by trust networks partly beyond its direct control. For example, local priests, schoolteach- ers, and administrators were often recruited and/or hired locally, and their loyalty tended to be mixed. Simultaneously, the decentralized man- agement of state authority that took place in local courts and municipal institutions was not only characterized by a mixed loyalty of the same kind; it also formed the institutional basis for opposition of a more organized, political type, potentially to be played out within the insti- tutional framework of the state itself. It seems highly fruitful, along the lines spelled out by Stenius (2010), Knudsen (2000), and Sørensen and Stråth (1997), to view this dynamic in the context of a dominant world- view and language of Protestant Lutheranism, privileging individual discipline, modesty, and organization. In the Norwegian context at least, in hindsight it seems logical that the first serious controversy between the state/church and the popular movements that challenged its authority was about the right to congregate and to speak freely in such contexts, as well as the freedom to establish businesses, to which I later return.

Barnes' second point, noted above, about the emerging class system, provides another means of approaching the same general process. In my own view, Barnes is but one among a large number of scholars who have failed to acknowledge the penetrating nature of protoindustrial capitalism in premodern Scandinavia, and its effects on identities, class relations, and political mobilization. The "peasants" Barnes observed were not late arrivals to the capitalist world market; they were, as was the case with the majority of farmers in Norway since the sixteenth century (particularly in areas not too far from the coast and major waterways), commercial agents and only involved in subsistence part-time (Østerud 1978). From 1500 to 1850, the population of Norway increased tenfold, but economic growth was even faster and stronger (Dyrvik 1979). Such a growth rate is exceptional in premodern economies. In the case of Norway, the most significant aspect of this may not be the growth rate as such, which clearly is related to the relative abundance of available resources such as fish, timber, metals, and available land to be cultivated, but rather its distribution. As resources were relatively easily available to common folk, the need for capital investments was rarely overwhelming. Moreover, some of the most promising commercial activities that grew in importance later in the period, especially shipping and ship brokering, were not to any great extent monopolized by the elites, even though they actively sought protection through royal privileges (which became outdated when economic liberalism gained hegemony in the early 1800s).

A large proportion of the freeholding farmers (who, since the Black Death, always constituted the majority, but were reduced somewhat during parts of the eighteenth century) in Norway found themselves in a favorable situation to exploit the opportunities provided by increasing demand, both in the international and in the internal market. According to economic historians Ståle Dyrvik (1979), Håvard Teigen (2006), one important factor here was the flexibility of their adaption. Subsistence activities were labor-intensive, but could be carried out by women ("deputy husbands," in the words of Solheim 2016), children, and the elderly when the men were away fishing, cutting and transporting timber, and so on. In periods of market failure, they could invest in more animals and intensify the use of available uncultivated land, often forest areas and grassland at higher altitudes. Because of this flexibility, taking part in commercial activities did not constitute a major risk. Microlevel specialization proved highly adaptable and profitable, and this may even help explain why the exceptional preindustrial growth was both strong and steady (Brox 1966; Dyrvik 1979: 237).

The political interests of Norwegian peasant farmers were profoundly shaped by their activities and identities as agents in commercial markets. Clearly such activities and identities also influenced their interest in other resources that became available in the predemocratic state, such as technology to be used for innovating agriculture, cutting and transporting wood/building materials, catching and preserving cod, herring, or trout, and, perhaps above all, the ability to read and write. Not surprisingly, much of the negotiations involving the state and farmers involved access to markets, protection of property, and taxes. There is little doubt that in the same way as the state (the royal sovereign) acknowledged its dependence on farmers as soldiers, it realized that the potential for tax revenue did not depend primarily on subsistence production but also on their role as producers and entrepreneurs in expanding markets. Probably for that reason there seems to have been a conscious policy from around 1670 to be careful not to tax the farmers too harshly (Dyrvik 1979: 251). "The King's weakness was his strength," Norwegian historian Magne Njåstad has pointed out, referring to the attempts to establish a foundation for legitimacy on the part of the king and the state in the late Middle Ages. As result of establishing this foundation on premises already established in local institutions, the state became mainly a guarantee of the status quo (Njåstad 2003: 250; Dørum 2010). It should be noted here that these institutions, local courts in particular, represented a deep-seated tradition of formal judicial–political negotiation reaching back to Viking times (Titlestad 2016).

THE DYNAMICS OF POLITICAL CHANGE IN SCANDINAVIA

The political organization of Scandinavia in the eighteenth century was quite diverse. Denmark was an "absolute" monarchy with a deeply feudal countryside, Norway its colony, and Sweden a former military great power with a strong centralist state and a rather "un-Western European" mooring in the peasantry (Knudsen and Rothstein 1994; Østergård 1992; Stenius 2010). In cultural terms, their commonalities were above all related to Protestantism and the profound effects of the Reformation. As pointed out above, state and church became one, and in contrast to most other European countries, no alternative sources of authority competed with the political sovereign. This "theocratization" of society (the unity of state and church/religion), and construction of a "one-norm society" (Stenius 2010: 33), contributed significantly to marginalize the idea that society consists of incommensurable subcultures, and to pave the way for uniform institutions based on Protestant values. Moreover, it provided what Finnish historian Henrik Stenius calls "rigid, but effective practices of inclusion (on work, education, local government, and the production and dissemination of practical knowledge"; Stenius 2010: 31). However, although this institutional uniformity constituted a powerful mechanism for control and the imposition of discipline, and proved an extremely efficient means for governing the population according to the logic of what we may call "direct rule" (Tilly 1990) of an "indirect" kind, it was less successful in preventing the lower classes from using state institutions for their own purposes. Five aspects should be highlighted.

First, the class dynamics in Scandinavia were tense, and had strong effects on political conflicts long before democratization. The royal sovereign effectively outmaneuvered the aristocracy quite early on, and the peasantry became important as a supplier of soldiers and tax revenue. The urban bourgeoisie played an important role, but it was internally fragmented and its relationship with the state and the peasants remained complex, thus preventing it from becoming an all-dominant actor. In Norway, which is my main case study in this chapter, urban merchants and protoindustrialists depended heavily on the king to protect their privileges (from the fourteenth century to the nineteenth), but also on peasant farmers, who were in control of much of the timber (and supplied the fish). Political conflicts in the autocratic state reveal complex patterns of alliances between these three sets of actors.

Second, political conflicts—at least from the mid-eighteenth century onwards—were nearly always about conflicting economic interests related to the key role of "part-time peasants" in expanding markets. A significant number of urban merchants, shippers, and protoindustrialists were formerly successful peasant farmers who had moved to town and specialized their business, and most of those who did not make this move were active in the timber trade.

The third factor that helped enable the lower classes to use state institutions for their own purposes was the nature of their political action.

Although often seen as deeply provocative and dangerous, political action on the part of the peasant farmers was generally of a highly disciplined and well-organized kind, based on experience from decision making in local communities. Faced with such a degree of organization, the authorities actively reflected upon their own possibility whether to respond with "the policy of the iron fist" (Sejersted 2003) and attempts at domestication.

Fourth, throughout Scandinavia, municipalities were relatively autonomous but at the same time heavily involved in dealing with the interests of the state locally. Municipalities were not task-specific, but generalist (especially after the municipal laws issued in 1837), and partly due to the broad scope of their activity, the boundaries between them as elected bodies, on the one hand, and voluntary associations, were not always very clear (Stenius 2010: 39). Social control in the local community was not simply limited to controlling the governed or those governing, mutual and multiplex. It also worked through a sense of equal membership that became strongly reinforced as voluntary organizations became politicized and in part co-opted by the state.

The fifth factor concerns patterns of social differentiation. From the early nineteenth century onwards, it became common for individuals to be members of several associations. The organizational landscape thus became extraordinarily complex and overlapping, although uniform in its institutional structure and scope. Most movements and organizations had their basis in local communities, organized members formally, operated according to strict procedures, and were joined together in umbrella organizations nationally. They not only took responsibility for one section of society, but sought comprehensive policy solutions and did not see themselves as outside the state (Stenius 2010: 51; Knudsen and Rothstein 1994).

CHALLENGES TO STATE POWER: SOME EXAMPLES OF POLITICAL MOBILIZATIONS AND THEIR AFTERMATH

The Lofthus Rebellion

In the 1780s and 1790s, a major uprising took place in Southern Norway, the so-called "Lofthus Rebellion," popularly understood as a "peasant rebellion." Its initiator was Jørgen Lofthus, who was frustrated by what he saw as unlawful behavior on the part of local state officials as well as by merchants in the town of Arendal, one of many coastal towns with an extremely vibrant economy (Dyrvik and Feldbæk 1996; Fiskaa 2012). He was able to collect considerable amounts of documentation before anyone tried to stop him, and mobilized large numbers of allies among peasant farmers in the south. He and his followers claimed that officials and merchants alike broke the rules of the game as established by the king, and one of the first things he did was in fact to go to Copenhagen to attempt to deliver his complaint to the sovereign in person. At one point, thousands of followers were ready to march to Christiania, the capital, to confront the officials seen as responsible. The uprising became too much for the authorities, however, and was put down, eventually landing Lofthus and some of his followers in jail (where he himself died). During the uprising, which was a wholly nonviolent affair, a range of conflicting interests was involved. First, Lofthus himself was a successful entrepreneur and involved in shipping with timber, in addition to owning a small farm. His frustration with the local merchants mainly concerned one merchant pointing out that other merchants in the same town enjoyed and abused privileges. In his attacks on local authorities, Lofthus surely had many of these same merchants behind him. The peasants who joined his movement were not marginalized people ready to take desperate action, but mostly farmers who were fully able to document their complaints and appeal to the law in order to protect their economic interests (related to the timber trade in particular).

The reaction the uprising eventually triggered was severe in several ways, but it resulted in the establishment of a commission that ended up debating the need for reforms, most notably in the area of economic liberalization. Economic liberalization was one of the most important elements in Lofthus' program, but now it was formulated in even broader terms than he himself had done. Especially in the higher strata of the state bureaucracy, the uprising inspired a concern with corruption at the local level and a more positive attitude to the lower classes as political actors (Dyrvik and Feldbæk 1996: 65). The process, most probably illustrating a deeper set of common interests between the peasant farmers as entrepreneurs and agents of economic change (and growth) and the state (the king), recurred in Denmark half a century later. As Danish agriculture lost out in the competition in the increasingly internalized grain market, and Danish farmers initiated changing production strategies from plants to livestock, the associational infrastructure that made this possible was supported by the state (mainly for military and economic reasons), even in periods of deeply conservative rule (Østergård 1992; Kaspersen and Ottesen 2001: 114).

The Haugians

Only a few years after the Lufthus Rebellion, another grassroots movement grew to great proportions in Norway, encompassing large parts of the country (Dyrvik and Feldbæk 1996; Dørum 2010; Grytten 2013). Hans Nielsen Hauge, a religiously devoted Puritan farmer from the southeast corner bordering Sweden, began a "grand tour" as a preacher and modernizer. He gathered people to preach a form of anticlerical Lutheranism promoting the (well-known) idea that each man is directly responsible to God, that official mediators do not have a legitimate place in this dyad, and that the path to salvation consists of disciplined conduct. By bringing common people together, preaching the Gospel, and educating them in agricultural innovation, business development, and the ability to read and write, Hauge provoked the representatives of the state, who feared that this could lead towards freedom of assembly and political opposition. Hauge himself was moderate in his provocations, but consistent in pursuing his entrepreneurial religiosity among people, and he was extremely successful in both regards.

After having been active for about ten years, he was arrested in 1804. Those most provoked by him and the movement were the church, which was an important part of the local state bureaucracy, but also many urban merchants, who saw his business orientation, and the increasing numbers of competitors resulting from his teaching, as a threat to their interests (as holders of commercial privileges). Businesses established by Hauge and his followers included paper mills, paper factories, salt processing plants, shipyards, provision of fishing vessel equipment, fish preservation (smoking, drying, salting), copper mining, shipping, and printing houses (Grytten 2013: 36). In much the same way as the authorities reacted to Lofthus' activities, they ended up treating him with greater leniency than might have been expected. Again, the alliance whose voice became decisive consisted of higher officials and a large portion of all those who could profit from increasing liberalization of the economy. Indeed, Hauge's entrepreneurship had clearly demonstrated that there could be an alternative to the traditional way of collecting revenue (through urban privileges), and a means to stimulate economic growth without losing control. Presumably as a result of this, Hauge's movement began to fascinate leading officials, who chose to express publicly that he was in many ways a respectful man whose morality and discipline were undisputed. Shortly after his death in 1824, it became common for successful entrepreneurs in Norway to call themselves "Haugians".

The Menstad Battle

The largest and most important industrial confrontation between labor and capital in large-scale industry occurred in 1931, at Menstad in the town of Skien (also located in the southeast of Norway; Kjeldstadli 1994; Berntsen 2014). As a result of the economic crisis, the employer in the town (Hydro, which at the time specialized in producing salpeter), decided that they needed to cut wages, and when the workers rejected accepting this, the company initiated a total lockout. They recruited strikebreakers with impunity, arguing that because there was not a strike but a lockout there could be no strikebreaking. The workers kept guard and for almost a month prevented workers from entering the plant. The cabinet minister of defense, the infamous Vidkun Quisling (who later became the Führer of Norway during the German occupation, and a major international symbol of national betrayal), sent a group of military police and a warship to confront them. However, although the police fired one shot, the conflict ended peacefully. The heated national debate that followed nevertheless inspired some fear that a revolution was imminent. Knut Kjeldstadli, one of many historians who have written about the subject, states that "[T]he conflict ended with a draw" (1994: 184). The employers did not succeed in their attempts to cut wages; in fact the workers ended up with a higher wage than the average in most other comparable countries. Shortly after the confrontation, workers' rights were also strengthened in several areas, institutionalized through the "Main Agreement" between the employers' union and the labor movement's foremost organization, the LO (*Landsorganisasjonen*, The National Union), and four years later the first Labor government was established, based on a political agreement with the party Quisling had represented as cabinet minister during "the Menstad Battle" in 1931. In hindsight, it seems clear that the Norwegian labor movement was never radically anticapitalist. It recruited almost all of its members more or less directly from the farming population, which is to say from people intensely interested in, among other things, protecting private property.

Also of relevance here is the conservative–liberal approach to fascism in this period in Norway, which reflects a general Scandinavian pattern. All the major parties on the right ended up rejecting the fascist movement, thereby channeling authoritarian sensibilities and interests towards moderate political programs. One general insight that can be drawn from this is that the political interests of conservative–liberal elites in Norway, who had struggled hard to contain political opposition from the left and democratization more generally, were seen by the same elites as best served by the strategy of nonconfrontation (Sejersted 2005). At this time, there was little doubt that political power had to rest on electoral support, and these parties had no significant independent electoral base beyond that which was increasingly mobilized by the social democrats.

POLITICAL MOBILIZATION: SOME PRELIMINARY CONCLUSIONS

From these historical illustrations of political conflict leading to, and resulting from, political mobilization, some patterns emerge. There is no doubt that the experience of social class was a foundational reason why the conflicts took place. However, from a European perspective, the kinds of interests involved, the institutional context in which they were negotiated, and the alliances (and political "consensus") established during the process constituted peculiar features of political contests and compromise. In fact, state authorities ended up *not* responding to potentially authority-threatening political mobilization by extending the definition of criminal behavior. All examples involve some form of initial concessions followed by reform. Furthermore, in all three cases the initiators and their followers were able to gain from unstable class alliances. This involved, among other things, some elite interests that could somehow benefit from possible change. In addition to this, and perhaps most importantly, the authorities' tendency to choose the path of domesticating opposition meant—at least in the long run—that the state apparatus (partly through the political parties) extended its scope and incorporated the associations organizing the opposition through corporatist arrangements. One significant aspect of this was that in doing so, it also made itself vulnerable to the mobilizing capacity of the associations that were invited to play a role in decision making. The major associations became in part an integral part of the state, and tended to maintain and reproduce their organizational form, founded in the idea of membership across social class divisions and regional boundaries (and, we may add, in both town and country). Finally, as Stenius (2010) has pointed out, one of the key "ideological" visions shared by many of these associations, the idea of universalism, gradually became an important premise for policy.

FOUR PHASES OF STATE BUILDING

To sum up, we may fruitfully see the trajectory of Norwegian state building as a process of four successive, partly overlapping phases. This categorization may help us highlight an analytical dimension of vital importance in this book. The Scandinavian welfare state is not a product of a broad consensus enabling state elites to design policy according to a consistent ideological horizon, nor is it a process of progressive modernization. Primarily it is a political struggle between organized, shifting, and more or less overlapping interests that mobilized alliances from which policy initiatives, compromise, and waves of institutionalization emerged. In comparative terms, one significant aspect of this process was the force of local experiences, experiments, and alliances, and the need for state rulers to adapt to them. The relative power of state elites, on the one hand, and locally based movements and interests, has shifted, generating highly contradictory institutional arrangements and shifting alliances with long-term, largely unintended consequences.

In Charles Tilly's grand comparative analysis of the development of European states, ambitiously and clearly spelled out in *Capital and Coercion in European States AD. 900–1990* (1990), the early Scandinavian states differed from both capital-driven and coercion-driven European neighbors. Unlike Italian city states, England, and Holland, the Swedish and Danish states depended less on powerful merchant and early industrial capital classes. However, landlordism was also less dominant, and the royal sovereign early established strong links directly to the peasant masses, mainly due to the need for taxes and soldiers. Because of the specific effects of the reformation in Scandinavia, this relationship became much more important than in the rest of Europe. First, it is significant to note that apart from being unusually direct, the amalgamation of state and church created a highly unitary, but at the same time broad domain of contact and negotiation. For example, Protestant priests were often appointed locally and performed state functions on a broad basis, organizing not only religious activity but also activities related to education, health, and agricultural innovation. Although this "protobureaucratic" organization of relationships between state rulers and local people was of course deeply hierarchical, its efficiency rested on more or less continuous negotiation, which not only concerned the size of taxes but also the actual performance of state officials. The pressure exercised by local communities to get rid of officials who developed tax farming (private tax revenue collection) businesses and other types of manipulation that threatened them, had interesting effects in two ways, not least because it could serve the royal sovereign well in extracting resources and get rid of competitors. It mobilized farmers and created an infrastructure of political organization and contention, and helped develop widely shared ideas of noncorrupt government. This direct form of rule was, however, also partly indirect, not in the sense of being mediated by local landlords, but rather well-established local forms of self-government.

Second, and perhaps even more interesting, the tax base to which this arrangement enabled royal rulers to gain access was considerable. In Norway in particular, especially from the sixteenth century onwards, economic growth was significant and largely driven by yeomen farmers, who had direct access to raw material (timber, in particular) that was not monopolized by urban merchants or landlords. From 1660 onwards, when the Danish king formally established absolutism, state rule became much more powerful, but its logic largely remained. Yeomen farmers had to yield much influence to both rising urban merchants benefiting from royal privileges, and the state bureaucracy. However, the tax burden was relatively light, property relations were not radically altered, and in the nineteenth century, the new ideology of economic liberalism provided farmers with a new sense of autonomy and direct access to markets.

The second phase, covering most of the eighteenth and nineteenth centuries up until 1914, when Norway established its own liberal democratic constitution, may be labeled the bureaucratic phase proper. Although characterized by an almost explosive political mobilization, I emphasize "bureaucratic" for two reasons. First, Danish rule was to a very great extent "Prussian" (Knudsen and Rothstein 1994). It became increasingly autonomous. In Norway, after the separation with Denmark in 1814 and immediate inclusion in the "union" with Sweden, this was experienced as an authoritarian backlash in relation to the great hopes and optimism inspired by the Constitution. The country was ruled by a powerful, yet not very big, state bureaucracy obsessed with its own integrity and power. It was torn between Norwegian political nationalism and reformism, on the one hand, and by the increasing frustration on the part of the Swedish King due to the troublesome Norwegian

National Assembly, *Stortinget*. Partly as a result of this, the rule of law became salient and the major battleground between the two opposing interests.

The third phase covers *The Social Democratic Era* (Sejersted 2005) from 1935 to around 1980–1990. Although hardly a precise term or a clearly delineated period, the change it brought about in terms of the logics of rule cannot be ignored. The Norwegian Labor Party, greatly inspired by the social reform program initiated by the previous liberal governments seizing governmental power after the separation from Sweden in 1905, built a new kind of state. Welfare reforms, broadly understood, involved an extreme mobilization of the population into the labor market, both in the expanding industrial as well as the public sector. The growth of public services was an extraordinarily labor-intensive business, and the state absorbed an increasing number of street-level bureaucrats, especially in the municipalities. Almost all of them were educated and hired locally, and entered a hybrid bureaucratic system influenced both by the Prussian type of autonomous state bureaucracy, and local communalism. Through the whole period of almost unlimited expansion, the steadily increasing number of municipal bureaucrats, service providers, and politicians tended to see themselves as servants of the state, but perhaps primarily as local agents and representatives of their own communities. The central state's direct control over these categories of actors was mainly limited to providing directions as to what services to extend, as opposed to how to organize them or provide them. The state was much less concerned with directly influencing the level and quality of services, ways of exerting professional discretion, and the management of municipal budgets. Indeed, the state did not constitute a system of direct rule. However, partly because of the enormous support for the expansion of the welfare state, as well as the lack of heavy investment in bureaucratic control, it proved highly efficient. The municipalization of the state went a long way, and in several respects, this helped make the central state mainly into a coordinating office. "Weberian anarchy" may be a way to characterize the extraordinary postwar welfare state expansion in Scandinavia. Its bureaucratic setup was based on "the principle of fixed and official jurisdictional areas, which are generally ordered by rules, that is, by laws and administrative regulations" (Weber 1946, in Fukuyama 1996: 222). One important consequence of its mooring in general rules was that "the ability of superiors to have their way was limited" (ibid.). Although "the rights and duties of service providing institutions were spelled out in advance" (ibid.), these rights and duties were at the same time deeply shaped by the utopian vision inherent in welfare state universalism, establishing as a general principle that the attention to needs, not budgets, constitutes the basic frame of reference. This may help explain why citizen rights in the Scandinavian welfare state have largely been understood in literal terms, as opposed to being seen as symbols of political competition.

I choose to label the fourth phase of the construction of state rule in Norway *the managerial, corporate, and performative turn* (Kapferer and Bertelsen 2009), however, as indicated above, with a twist. The combination of the ideologically driven economic liberalization and privatization and the panic among state elites stirred by a seemingly uncontrollable public sector, stimulated the growth of a new managerial system of leadership and control, subsumed under symbolic categories such as "efficiency" and "government by objectives." However, the systematic centralization and hierarchicalization of the public sector since the 1990s has not implied a parallel reduction of political ambitions to pursue ambitious programs of welfare state expansion. Drawing on insights from political science and historical sociology it would appear that the managerial corporate turn came too late. The institutionalization of the welfare state may have gone too far. For example, the process of decommodification has deeply influenced identities, as people's experience of autonomy is closely connected with having access to public services, and political alliances supporting municipal service provision has grown strong. Local patriotism in municipal politics generally expresses itself as a defense of the welfare municipality, and tends to unite local politicians across party boundaries, as well as municipal employees, user organizations, and other voluntary associations.

At any rate, I draw attention to the consequences of the parallel process of increasing welfare state ambitions and austerity, which most profoundly affect the relationship between the central state and the municipalities. This is what I refer to by labeling the emergent state form as not only managerial and corporate, but also performative. As a part of the attempt to construct direct links to, and seek the support and loyalty from, citizens and "users," welfare policy tends to take the form of individual rights, which in turn become the major mechanism whereby state elites control the performance of service providers. As the latter become overwhelmed by responsibility that they lack the capacity to meet, state elites enter a position that allows them to perform as heroes of good intentions and the allies of unhappy users vis-à-vis bureaucrats and service providers. In the shadow of this performance, public institutions and their services are becoming less accessible and informal means testing is expanding rapidly. The bureaucratic Taylorism emerging from this dynamic is characterized by increasingly detailed and legalistic forms of control, which in turn inspire demands from the service-providing levels of public institutions to specify duties and responsibilities. Because the message is that trust is not an option, there is a growing need for more detailed rules, so that it becomes possible for differently positioned actors to protect themselves from each other.

The trajectory described here, by means of my classification of four phases of state rule is *not* a modernization narrative. Although modernization theory at its best may help us map some key patterns of long-term change in processes of democratization, and its relation to capitalism, individualization, and bureaucratic institutions, its teleological view prevents us from taking seriously the contingencies involved in political power struggles and their potential for generating "de-democratization" (Tilly), "oligarchy" (Kapferer and Bertelsen), and "political decay" (Fukuyama).

> Elites tend to get more entrenched because they can use their wealth, power, and social status to get access to the government, and to use the power of the state to protect themselves and their children. This process will continue until nonelites succeed in mobilizing politically to reverse or otherwise protect themselves. (Fukuyama 2014: 57)

The relative power of nonelites to prevent elites from "retraditionalizing" politics and institutions is becoming an issue of vital importance, and constitutes a key factor in any attempt to explain why Western democracies have taken such different routes after the financial crisis in 2007. In this book I make a systematic attempt to explore historically how, in Scandinavia and Norway in particular, nonelites have operated in order to prevent elites from monopolizing access to government.

REFERENCES

Barnes, J. 1954. Class and Committees in a Norwegian Island Parish. *Human Relations* 7 (1): 39–58.

Berntsen, H. 2014. Det røde fylket. In *Telemarks historie*, vol. 3, ed. Rovde et al., 197–217. Bergen: Fagbokforlaget.

Brox, Ottar. 1966. *Hva skjer i Nord-Norge? En studie i norsk utkantpolitikk.* Oslo: Pax.

Dørum, K. 2010. Opprør eller legitim politisk praksis? Kommunalisme og folkelige aksjoner i Norge ca. 1700–1850. In *Demokratisk teori og historisk praksis. Forutsetninger for folkestyre 1750-1850*, ed. Sandvik, H, 71–105. Oslo: Spartacus.

Dyrvik, S. 1979. *Norsk økonomisk historie 1500-1970*, 1: 1500–1850. Bergen: Universitetsforlaget.

Dyrvik, S., and O. Feldbæk. 1996. Mellom brødre 1780-1830. In *Norges historie*, vol. 7, ed. K. Helle. Oslo: Aschehoug.

Fiskaa, Ingrid. 2012: *Lofthusreisinga i Agder og Telemark 1786-87*, in Opptøyer i Norge ed. Dørum, K. & Sandvik, H.: 1750-1850. Oslo: Spartacus.

Fukuyama, Francis. 1996. *Trust. The Social Virtues and the Creation of Prosperity.* New York: Simon & Schuster.

Fukuyama, F. 2011. *The Origin of Political Order: From Prehuman Times to the French Revolution.* New York: Farrar, Strauss and Giroux.

Fukuyama, Francis. 2014. *Political Order and Political Decay: From the Industrial Revolution to the Globalisation of Democracy.* London: Profile Books.

Graubard, Stephen R. (ed.). 1986. *Norden: The Passion for Equality.* Oslo: Norwegian University Press.

Grytten, O. 2013. The Protestant Ethic and the Spirit of Capitalism: Entrepreneurship of the Norwegian Puritan Leader Hans Nielsen Hauge. *Review of European Studies* 5 (1): 31–44.

Kaspersen, Lars B, and Laila Ottesen. 2001. Associationalism for 150 years and still alive and kicking: Some reflections on danish civil society. *Critical Review of International and Political Philosophy*, 4 (1): 105–130.

Kjeldstadli, Knut. 1994. Et splittet samfunn. In *Norges historie*, vol. 10, ed. K. Helle. Oslo: Aschehoug.

Knudsen, T., and Bo Rothstein. 1994. State Building in Scandinavia. *Comparative Politics* 26 (2): 203–220.

Knudsen, Tim. 2000. Inledning. In *Den nordiske protestantisme og velfærdsstaten*, ed. Tim Knudsen, 7–20. Aarhus: Aarhus Universitetsforlag.

Njåstad, M. 2003. *Grenser for makt Konflikter og konfliktløsning mellom lokalsamfunn øvrighet ca. 1300-1540.* PhD thesis, Trondheim, Institutt for historie og klassiske fag, NTNU.

Østergård, U. 1992. Peasants and Danes: The Danish National Identity and Political Culture. *Comparative Studies in Society and History* 34 (1): 3–27.

Østerud. 1978. *Peasant Politics in Scandinavia. A Comparative Study of Rural Response to Economic Change.* Oslo: Universitetsforlaget.

Sejersted, Francis. 2003. *Opposisjon og posisjon. Høyres historie 1945-1981*. Oslo: Cappelen.

Sejersted, Francis. 2005. *Sosialdemokratiets tidsalder: Norge og Sverige i det 20. århundre*. Oslo: Pax.

Skirbekk, G. 2010. *Norsk og moderne*. Oslo: Res Publica.

Solheim, J. 2016. Bringing it all Back Home–familien som generativ kulturell formasjon i det moderne. *Norsk antropologisk tidsskrift* 27 (1): 7–21.

Sørensen, Øystein, and Bo Stråth. 1997. *The Cultural Construction of Norden*. Oslo: Scandinavian University Press.

Stenius, Henrik. 2010. Nordic Associational Life in a European and an Inter-Nordic Perspective. In *Nordic Associations in a European Perspective*, ed. Henrik Stenius and Risto Alapuro. Baden-Baden: Nomos.

Stråth, Bo. 2005: *Union og demokrati–dei sameinte rika Norge-Sverige 1814-1905*. Oslo: Pax.

Teigen, Håvard. 2006. Bønder flest er ikkje forretningsmenn? *Historisk tidsskrift* 83 (1): 107–120.

Tilly, Charles. 1990. Coercion, Capital and European States, A. D. 990–1990. Cambridge: Cambridge University Press.

Tilly, Charles. 2005. *Trust and Rule*. Cambridge: Cambridge University Press.

Titlestad, T. 2016. *Vikingtid: Motstandsrett og folkestyre*. Stavanger: Saga Bok.

Vike, Halvard. 2012. Varianter av vest-europeiske statsformasjoner–Utkast til en historisk antropologi. *Norsk antropologisk tidsskrift* 23 (2): 126–142.

Vike, H. 2015. Likhetens natur. *Norsk antropologisk tidsskrift* 25 (1): 7–21.

Weber, Max. 1946. *From Max Weber. Essays in Sociology*. Oxford/New York: Oxford University Press.

CHAPTER 6

Borders, Boundaries, and Bureaucratic Reform

The Performance of Public Institutions

The last couple of decades have brought a remarkable increase in the interest in state performance, including a crossdisciplinary fascination for how public institutions actually work, and what that means in terms of the legitimacy of the state (Kumlin 2004; Kapferer and Bertelsen 2009; Fukuyama 2011, 2014; Rothstein 2011). Bo Rothstein, a major inspiration in this field of scholarly work, notes [with reference to the work of Theda Skocpol (1992)] that:

> ... [T]he United States welfare state was comparatively well developed at the beginning of the twentieth century, but was thereafter politically delegitimized owing to what was generally perceived as its low quality of government. (Rothstein 2011: 126)

> Staffan Kumlin has shown that citizens' direct experience from interacting with various social policy programs has a clear influence on their political opinions. Moreover, such experiences are more important than citizens' personal economic circumstances when they form opinions about supporting welfare state policies. (Kumlin 2004: 199–200; in Rothstein 2011: 126)

As far as explaining the actual performance of public institutions is concerned, Swedish/Greek sociologist Apostolis Papakostas' analysis of bureaucratic traditions in Sweden, "Why Is There No Clientelism

© The Author(s) 2018   111
H. Vike, *Politics and Bureaucracy in the Norwegian Welfare State*,
Approaches to Social Inequality and Difference,
https://doi.org/10.1007/978-3-319-64137-9_6

in Sweden?" is an interesting case in point. With an analytical inspiration drawn from historical sociology (Stein Rokkan and Charles Tilly in particular), Papakostas asks how public institutions became socially embedded in Swedish society. One key factor, he argues, is the historical relationship between state building, capitalist expansion, and democratization. In Sweden, the institutions of the (strong) state were well established before democratic mass mobilization took place, and the capitalist transformation as well as mass education had contributed heavily to a thorough individualization of society. In the democratization process, there was virtually no room for patrons and other powerful mediators, and in sociological terms political representation and power came to rest on individual membership in associations, whereas state institutions dealt with the population qua individuals classified bureaucratically as members of general categories. According to Papakostas, the ultimate contrast in the European context may be Greece, where the modern state was largely incorporated into informal structures of authority and loyalty. In Sweden, the state bureaucracy grew strong during a period of exceptional autonomy.

One of the fascinating themes in Papakostas' discussion is how complex bureaucracies at the local level, responsible for organizing and providing a wide array of services, could actually function in very small-scale contexts without becoming absorbed by informal power relations. According to Papakostas, the historical (and partly accidental) timing is essential. For example, as the street-level bureaucracy grew strong and became a key feature of the state, the discretion that had to be practiced in the interface between the state and local populations could be appropriated from bureaucratic traditions stemming from the time of the monarchical *rechtstaat*. At a more general level, the peculiar adaptation of the street-level bureaucrats in the Scandinavian welfare state is yet to be explained (although Papakostas' discussion is a significant contribution). As representatives of ambitious welfare institutions with a strong tradition for professional autonomy and discretion, they have carried out their work in a world of conflicting loyalties and identities. As representatives of the users (as their advocates), local communities, their own professions, and their employers (the municipalities), they have, together with local political representatives in the municipal assemblies, played an important role as representatives with a double agenda.

Reforming the Municipal Organization

In the following, I explore this type of complexity as it unfolded in the context of a municipal reform process that aimed at establishing better control of welfare policy. It took place in Skien, where in 1994, politicians, leading administrators, and welfare workers joined efforts and formed a group that set out to launch a reorganization program that was to provide "better service for less money" to welfare clients (Vike 1996; Kronenfeld and Vike 2002). These three categories of participants, however, each understood the process and their own participation in it in different terms, and each had his or her point of view changed during the reorganization process. These changes and their consequences constitute the focus of attention in the present discussion. Although the point of departure of the three categories of actors was highly different, there was general agreement on the practical strategy that was developed. However, the parties' interpretations of the state of affairs after the project had been completed were again divergent and mutually contradictory.

The different perspectives held by the three parties involved must be seen in relation to the different tasks they were assigned in the municipal organization and to the positions from which they experience their environment and look for problems to be solved. Above all, they differed in the way in which they defined risk, that is, threats to the immediate environment within which they operated. In this project, politicians were pragmatically concerned with controlling the organization and reducing costs. From their point of view, welfare workers were potentially disloyal and clients irresponsible. Although such a view was most openly expressed by the elite politicians who took part in the project, the other, politically appointed or elected members seemed to see this as a regrettable fact of life and thus a premise for action. Welfare workers, on the other hand, generally tended to identify with their clients and regard politicians and leading administrators as more or less ignorant of the deep social and individual problems welfare clients represent. Welfare workers therefore saw politicians in particular as a threat to the meaningfulness of social work. Leading administrators were "betwixt and between." They tended to take a suspicious stand towards politicians because of the politicians' alleged "lack of responsibility" regarding the problems engendered by responses to economic scarcity. At the same time, they were aware of the interest that welfare workers had in protecting their autonomy and their domains, and leading administrators were thus concerned with the lack of financial responsibility into which such workers, in their desire to serve their clients, could fall.

These contrasting conceptualizations of the field contributed to a very ambiguous collective definition of the object of municipal welfare policies. The actors disagreed on what a welfare client really is and on what such a client really needs. Hence, as we show, a major part of the job was to achieve an understanding of the object that was sufficiently unambiguous to lend itself to operationalization. In other words, inasmuch as the project aimed at effectively and efficiently changing the state of affairs, it had to be practical.

As shown in Chap. 3, the head of the civil service hierarchy is the *rådmannen* who reports directly to the Assembly. Under the *rådmannen* are the three chief bureaucrats (directors). These people report administratively to the *rådmann* and have their performance evaluated by him or her, but they provide administrative support for the three political committees (health and welfare, primary education and culture, and infrastructure, resp.) and interact frequently with committee members, and their job performance ratings are in part dependent on the committees' evaluation of the quality of their services. At a yet lower administrative level are the mid-level bureaucrats who, of course, are also dependent on the effectiveness with which those under them function. Budgetary responsibility represents a major pressure on the bureaucrats, but responsibility for the quality of services their units deliver is also salient. Under the mid-level bureaucrats are the grass-roots bureaucrats—that is, in the case of the health and welfare committee, the health service professionals who actually deliver the public services—the doctors, nurses, social workers, elder-care workers, and so forth who directly interact with the clients.

During the spring of 1994, the reorganization program, which was called *Bedre bruk av sosialhjelpsmidler* ("More adequate use of welfare funds," hereafter "the BB-project") was discussed extensively by a supervision group (*styringsgruppa*) consisting of leading politicians, administrative personnel, and welfare workers. The supervision group evaluated a pilot project that had been carried out over a four-year period in one of the municipality's three welfare offices. As a means for improving its performance, the office had been endowed with considerable special financial support, and the group was to find out whether the project had been successful. Had the welfare office been able to give more welfare clients adequate and relevant help? Furthermore, did more personnel, more efficient routines, and a stronger emphasis on rehabilitation of clients, as opposed to just helping them keep their heads above water, demonstrate a potential for reducing costs in the future? These questions were formulated on the basis of a perspective on administrative governance inspired by "government by objectives" logic. The relationship between goals and the means at hand was essential, and in part defined by the model applied, "Quality Pays". According to the evaluation report, "The main idea in the project is based on a connection between the quality of professional work and the welfare payments ('quality pays')."

The group had a very hard time reaching conclusions. The results as presented in the report were very ambiguous. Despite the improved personnel situation, the office in question had in fact been far less successful in terms of controlling payments and exercising budget discipline than had the other two offices that had not been endowed with special privileges or resources. Moreover, the discrepancy between client needs and the welfare office's performance had grown, particularly as far as rehabilitation work was concerned (i.e., the proportion of clients weaned from rehabilitation support fell rather than rose). However, the welfare workers on their part regarded the project as partly successful. They reported that they enjoyed their work more than before, evincing better morale and job satisfaction. Furthermore, they had been able to organize their work more adequately, achieve better control, and felt that they were actually giving more meaningful help to something closer to the full range of citizens who needed such help; they felt that their lowered statistical success rate in fact represented a situation in which they were finally able actually to engage the real problems instead of having to push them aside or only marginally deal with them.

From the start the social workers had been extremely hesitant to accept the ambition to achieve better service for less money but, apparently because their relationship to the administration and leading politicians suffered from a serious legitimacy deficit as they were under suspicion of being the client's advocates rather than loyal municipal functionaries, they accepted the project's terms and opted for the potentially positive results of pragmatic cooperation. Yet the positive results, as the participants themselves saw it, had an ironic flavor, because the results had little to do with the overall goal of the project, which was to save money. The results, even the positive ones, were largely unintended and, from the focal perspective, extraneous. Some of the politicians and leading administrators were deeply dissatisfied, and one of them concluded bitterly that "quality does in fact not pay." Consequently, the participants looked for alternative ways to provide better services for lower costs. It was explicitly expressed that the project was in danger of becoming a collection of "mere words," that is, a matter of good intentions without adequate means of execution.

In a conference where organizational strategy was discussed with reference to the BB-project, held a few months after the project had been evaluated, the complex relationship between rational planning and desired effects was discussed in terms of "goal structures." It became clear that the various participants held strongly opposed views on the meaning and importance of organizational goal structures. Some thought, for instance, that what really matters is not the content of the various goals, but rather the ability to develop "a common vision" in the organization, whereas others were strongly focused on the objective correctness of particular goals within the overall goal structure. Others thought that the goal structure had to be linked to a "tool," that is, actual money channeled through realistic budgets, in order to be seriously considered. Still others were more concerned with the organization's ability to stimulate a dialogue and normative commitment among its members.

Despite the disagreement, an overall pragmatic consensus was achieved on the basis of the assumption that the ability to achieve organizational goals in practice depends on logical consistency among goals and on clearly formulated goal formulations and budget policies. Hence, this was what the rest of the conference was about. Repeatedly participants were provoked by speakers who uttered "mere words," that is, people who kept talking about intentions without making serious attempts to devise practical solutions. Such words, "better service for everyone" and "a secure life for everyone," were seen as almost meaningless because they didn't have procedures attached to them. They became "words on paper." Some participants were also provoked when it was suggested that factors other than just logical consistency and clearly formulated policies might influence organizational processes. For example, one of the speakers mentioned that organizational sabotage might prevent planned instrumental governance from becoming successful.

In the BB-project, two main roads to a better outcome were identified. One was to change the system according to which clients were classified, and another was to change the organization in order to make it more efficient. The first strategy resulted in the development of an informal classification of clients as "expensive" and "inexpensive" (in addition to an unmarked middle category) that could be used for deciding how to arrange the queue of clients waiting for measures so municipal costs could be reduced as quickly as possible. The second strategy generated a proposal for reorganization and was predicated on the idea that the initial reform failed because of a lack of administrative coordination and efficiency. This strategy rapidly became extremely controversial, and the welfare workers opposed it vehemently. The protests revealed a considerable amount of hostility towards the departmental leadership as well as towards the municipal leaders. One welfare worker identified the situation in the organization as a constant "war" about which no one ever dared speak. This echoed a general complaint among municipal service providers in Skien, a complaint that was expressed to me repeatedly in interviews, that leadership dominance is too great and that the meaningfulness of work is seriously threatened. However, although the others present agreed that the war metaphor was appropriate, no one opposed the overall strategy of which the reform attempt was a product: the attempt to increase control and efficiency.

It may be noted that the need for better service for less money through increasing organizational control was never challenged in the project, despite the fact that the overall goal of more service for less money clearly was not achieved. The failure was not in any way taken as an indication of a failed analysis or a failed policy; instead, it was taken as a failure of implementation, with the conclusion that what was needed were redoubled efforts along the lines which had just failed. In this sense the explanatory model held by the municipal administration seems to represent a self-fulfilling prophecy: no evidence can disconfirm it and apparently negative evidence serves only to reinforce it.

WHAT HAPPENED?

By what concepts and logic was this apparent failure rationalized and converted into a positive argument for the policy? The three categories of actors involved in the reorganization process understood the need to be practical and realistic, what we may call *paramount reality* (Berger and Luckmann 1967), that is, the point of reference to which all actions and experiences had to be related and via which, legitimated. The conclusion enabled actors to translate their ambiguous, and sometimes strikingly contradictory experiences, into a common operational discourse that, as they saw it, made it possible to translate strategy (as opposed to "mere words") into practices that may anticipate effects in an instrumental manner. What bridged the relationship between the three categories of actors, then, seems to be the way in which the organization as a collective embraced a frame of discourse that was sufficiently abstract for them all to buy into, and that thereby papers over the differences among their perspectives. The discourse frame worked most effectively, perhaps unsurprisingly, for those with the most power, who were, perhaps coincidentally, most removed from the problems of actual service for actual clients.

However, what in this case appeared on the surface to be a reform failure had some other effects, too, effects to which the actors did not pay much attention. The very fact that the reform did not realize the goal of saving money, was in a sense not at all bad news for the welfare workers and the many local politicians who identified with their role as representatives of "the weak ones in society" (which, as indicated in Chap. 3, was an expression in common use in Skien during my field-work). In fact, the failure to reduce expenses reflected a well-established practice among welfare workers to ignore restrictive, local welfare payment standards and instead conform to much more generous national guidelines. To defend this practice in times of economic crisis, they had established alliances with as many backbenchers in the Municipal Assembly as possible, as well as with the local media, so as to mobilize moral uproar when cutbacks "hit the weakest ones." As the welfare workers' chosen conformity to discourse of realism in the BB-project indicate, the welfare workers did not seem to problematize the apparent contradiction between what they seemed to say and what they seemed to do. Interestingly, it may be that precisely because they did not articulate this potential problem, but instead seemed to conform to whatever was in vogue among leading bureaucrats and politicians, that their "everyday resistance" was so effective. They were able to act collectively and consistently almost without any observable coordinating functions or articulated oppositional language. In this regard, the welfare workers illustrate a common phenomenon in municipal organizations in the ambitious Norwegian welfare state. As providers of welfare service, their mandate is to do everything they can to secure that people with rights to high-quality services actually receive them. This demands that grassroots bureaucrats be constantly on the lookout for problems to solve. On the other hand, they are supposed to be loyal to the municipal budget, which in order to stay balanced very often necessitates cutbacks. When caught in dilemmas of this kind, welfare workers, as other grassroots bureaucrats and many local politicians who do not identify with the political elites, are actually able to enter alliances with their users and the wider public, as well as with the central state. The latter insists through law that needs shall be met regardless of municipal budgets, yet at the same time insisting through law that municipal budgets be balanced.

Although economic considerations most often win, the analysis of the BB-project has shown that the municipal organization seems to have some built-in mechanisms that reproduced its "schizophrenic" nature. This organizational schizophrenia seems vital for the municipal organization's ability to take seriously the extremely complex task of being sensitive to shifting, growing, and ever more costly needs in the population. I have tried to show that it may be precisely because the actors themselves act, or at least talk, as though they think they can achieve control by applying some highly, perhaps overly simplified instrumental organizational model, that this is made possible. Their identity was strengthened, and their model of what they do together was simple enough to allow much of the substantial organizational work being left alone, unexplained, as it were. One important property of Norwegian municipalities is that they have hardly been effectively managed in the sense of being under someone's control, primarily because there are, or used to be, powerful actors within the organization who, through horizontal solidarity, are able to act according to standards other than those developed by managers (Deetz 1992; Du Gay 2000). As indicated in previous chapters, I think it is reasonable to assume that this may in part explain why municipalities are in fact highly successful providers of welfare services. Their success seems closely associated with a unique ability to modify negative effects of centralized leadership and managerial ambitions. How can we explain this?

OF ILLEGAL ALIENS AND BUREAUCRATS: AN ANALOGY

One of the central functions of bureaucracies is mobilizing and organizing knowledge. This knowledge is distributed within a hierarchically structured system of roles. As social systems, bureaucracies are characterized by the kind of tension present in any corporately organized group

of human beings: the tension between collective identity and corporate action and the individuals whose role-performances constitute the
organization. As far as the "thought work" in the welfare bureaucracy
is concerned, workers must think for themselves in order to get their
work done; at the same time organizational reproduction depends on the
ability to control their thinking (Heyman 1995). This tension is given
nourishment by the fact that public bureaucracies are often, as was the
case in the BB-project, simplistically or erroneously seen as instruments
that may be applied to produce effects. My point of departure is that
they are systems of social relations and governed by cultural conventions
(cultural norms and conventional links between signifiers, signifieds, and
referents).

A few years prior to the launching of the BB-project an organizational
conflict of considerable proportions occurred in the largest welfare office
in Skien. The conflict was defined by both parties involved—the administrative leadership and a large number of the employees in the department—as due to problems of cooperation. Apart from that, however, the
parties strongly disagreed on what was really the root of the problem as
well as how to solve it. As a result the conflict was formed as a tension
between two kinds of definitions. The subordinate employees sought
assistance from *bedriftshelsetjenesten* ("the health services for municipal
employees") and insisted that the deteriorated atmosphere in the department had created health problems, however, the leadership protested
and decided that the problem was purely "organizational" and argued
that "It is hard to see that the doctor is competent in this field."

A major problem for the municipal administration in issues of this
kind seemed to be related to the simple fact that "psychosocial problems" distorted the way it constructed its own units and boundaries.
Asking for the assistance of a doctor in this case was a way of suggesting
that the "real" organizational boundaries, as defined by the employees,
were to be found within each employee and not only between formally
defined bureaucratic slots. This action threatened not only the organizational design but also positions and, ultimately, the hierarchically organized system of knoweldge.

The more endangered the borders, the more intense the politics of identity are. This observation is the starting point for Michael Kearney's (1991)
study of the role of the US/Mexico border "at the end of empire" and in
the age of transnationalism. The flow of migrant workers across the border makes it apparent that there is an increasing "lack of correspondence

between the borders and boundaries of the nation-state" (ibid., 53). Kearney points to the fact that the border itself is really not at issue here, because migrants are indeed allowed to cross it. By utilizing the symbolic power potential of the physical border and the territoriality of the nation, the United States' *inscription of boundaries in individual persons* is made possible. The Border Patrol observes the migrants and the migrants know they are there, but most of the time no action is taken. According to Kearney,

> The nightscopes are but one component in a sophisticated hightech surveillance program that also incudes motion sensors, searchlights, television cameras, helicopters, spotter planes, and patrols in various kinds of boats and ground vehicles, all coordinated by computers and radio communications. The annual budget for this sector of the Border Patrol is millions of dollars, but no money has been allocated in recent years to repair the fence. (ibid., 57)

In this particular context, the overall goal of surveillance is seen by Kearney as the separation of two aspects of the individual person,

> to separate labor from the jural person within which it is embodied, that is, to disembody the labour from the migrant worker" (ibid., 58).

The migrants adapt to this process by allowing for the separation to be made. It is produced by the fear of being caught which, in turn, makes the migrants internalize the boundary. The example may serve us well as an analogy, because to a great extent modern politics and modern organizations deal with politics of identity and subjectivity. They do so in part by manipulating symbolic forms that influence employees' fear of crossing boundaries. In our example, organizational unity and efficiency are mediated by organizational routines, lines of command, work instructions, and budgets. The Border Patrol of the municipality of Skien, then, is the administrative and economic leadership which, through budget and information control, enforces the maintenance of organizational boundaries. By doing this it produces divisions, or boundaries, within individual employees that, in turn, are supposed to secure the loyalty upon which the ambition to control and use the organization as a tool depends.

ORDER AND DILEMMA: BUEAUCRATIC ROLES
AND MANEUVERABILITY

The leading administrators in Skien have close ties with the politicians, and most often they are the ones who experience political decisions most immediately. At the same time their position at the center of the formal information channels in the municipality gives them the possibility to influence these decisions. What they want from politicians is, above all, that they take responsibility and make decisions in ways that enable the administration to implement them. This is not a straightforward thing. For example, the administration often experiences that decisions lack realism, such as when resources are not available, when state regulations collide with them, or when they are too vague. How do they deal with this?

One leading administrator in Skien, who has experienced much pressure and turbulence during the last years, explains that she strives for a "streamlined" organization in which leaders are "responsible" and "loyal" and where information is "controlled." One major result of such an achievement will be to eliminate what she sees as an "artificial" contradiction between professional interests and the managers of the municipal economy. Thus what she wants to "deliver" to the politicians is an ordered governable organization. In return, she wants politicians to "make choices," to think in long terms and "understand their roles." As a result of her practical follow-up of this "deal," she has experienced quite a number of negative reactions from the politicians as well as from subordinates within her department. The most dramatic illustration of her somewhat tense relationship with the politicians was the HW committee meetings referred to in Chap. 3, when the disagreement on the budget procedures developed into a quarrel over her loyalty. As will be remembered, the politicians seriously doubted that she was loyal to the committee. To their surprise, she openly stated that in a sense she was not. Instead she had to follow the orders from her superior, *rådmannen*, whom she saw as the true representative of the political will as expressed in the long-term budget sanctioned by the Municipal Assembly.

Although the HW director does not always get along very well with the politicians in the committee, her interaction with the local political elite is much less tense. In this relationship there is a far broader agreement on the need to accept budgets and make choices. Yet she seems far from happy with the politicians' efforts, as she finds herself loaded with responsibility. When the task of making priorities is handed over to her by the politicians, the problem of legitimacy follows along with it and her authority within her own organization is put to the test. In the budget battle in 1993, for instance, she was able to prevent the open mobilization of her own subdepartment leaders and the politicians against her. The cost of her campaign, in terms of weakening of her own legitimacy, was no doubt considerable.

Two main goals seem to guide her and her colleagues at this level of the municipal bureaucracy: to eliminate scarcity and to clarify one's own responsibility. In return for unambiguous political decisions, as a part of the strategy to secure these overall values politicians are offered better plans, more thorough analyses, and greater administrative efficiency. In Chap. 3 I explored some aspects of this dynamic as it developed in the welfare sector in 1993. In the following I focus more closely on how this dynamic influences the way municipal employees understand their work situation.

The case of the HW director may serve as an example of a general problem in the relationship between political government and bureaucratic management. In Skien the overwhelming majority of politicians and bureaucrats agree that the basic problem is scarcity. For the HW director, one of the main frustrations is clearly that the politicians often fail to admit this, or at least fail to draw the necessary conclusions from this fact. And because administrative leaders lack the legitimacy necessary to enforce the follow-up of priorities that do not come with explicit political sanction, they have to find another solution. It seems to me that the prototypical example is looking inwards into the organization and seeking to eliminate scarcity and ambivalence through rationalization measures (Brunsson 1989; Brunsson and Olsen 1993). Because the legitimacy of the top level of the bureaucracy is constantly at stake, leadership legitimacy must be continually reaffirmed through demonstrations of control and efficiency, but the relations between top administrative leaders and their subordinates tend to make this very difficult.

Another leading administrator offers an interesting perspective on the problems in the HW department. He sees the controversy on loyalty in the HW department not as a strictly legal matter, but as an "ideological disagreement." In fact, he himself has not decided once and for all to whom he is loyal. Precisely because his loyalty is somewhat shifting according to changing circumstances, he seems to have no great hope that the loyalty problem will reach a final solution. For instance, he is very sceptical of what he calls "the strategic administrative thinking" which he thinks is strongly represented in Skien, particularly in the group of leading admnistrators (of which he is a part) that serves as the main consultative forum for *rådmannen*. A more pluralist approach to administration is more to his liking. "There's a balance between tolerance and order," he says. The attempts to "streamline" the organization, for instance, may prove harmful to the possibility to present politicians with real disagreements that exist within the bureaucracy. In his eyes the greatest danger is not necessarily the fragmentation of responsibility, which has been the main argument behind the streamlining process, but what he sees as a potentially "dangerous" alliance between the political elite and the top administrative level. Several times during my fieldwork this particular bureaucrat demonstrated an unusual professional independence and self-confidence in his interaction with elite politicians and fellow bureaucrats. He openly and clearly communicated disagreement and pursued prolonged verbal battles with them, even in the Municipal Council.

When moving one step down from the municipal administrative level the problems are to some degree similar, but nevertheless experienced quite differently. Here we encounter the heads of the various subdepartments. In the HW department, these lead the departments dealing with health care, refugees, social welfare, and housing, respectively. In the discussion of the budget controversy in 1993 (Chap. 3), I identified the contours of the problematic relationship between the politicians and the administration. The silence on the part of the subdepartment leaders was illlustrative of the new order that was about to be introduced. In part their interests ran directly counter to their leader; they tried to serve the politicians in their struggle to collect the arguments needed to be able to "fight elite politicians in all parties" but were prevented from doing so. In the committee meeting the politicians were provoked by the behavior of the director and directed their attention directly to her subordinates asking: "To whom are *you* loyal?" Although I am in no doubt that they all knew the answer and wanted to tell the politicians, no response was provided.

This stratum of leaders is betwixt and between in several ways, and their role can be characterized as highly ambiguous. They are translators par excellence, responsible for mediating between administrative functions and service provision, as well as for transforming policy and informal policy signals into practice. In addition, their position as subordinate administrators (vis-à-vis the director and the *rådmannen*) often makes it hard to handle the alliances they build with politicians; such alliances are unofficial and often remain hidden from the formal discourse. By education they are all professionals (welfare workers, nurses, doctors, etc.); their administrative tasks are added to a basic identification with specific segments of the welfare municipality and relative proximity to specific groups of people, both employees and client groups. They see themselves as spokespeople of certain professional values, and tend to feel alienated by the administrative language dominating among their superiors. The head of the largest subdepartment in the HW sector, *pleie- og omsorg*, ("care") feels that he must struggle hard to gain legitimacy for the work performed by his department.

> *Sentraladministrasjonen* ('the Central Administration') doesn't have the feeling for what happens in our sector. ... Economic considerations become more and more important.

Because he thinks that there is a general lack of trust between the different hierarchical levels of the organization, he feels the need to present the information concerning the conditions in his department to politicians and administrative superiors in new ways.

> Last year I started to break down information to the individual level, even if I ran the risk of becoming a social pornographer. If there was trust in the organization, that shouldn't be necessary.

"Break down information to the individual level" means, in this context, that in order to be heard he had to provide "evidence" that the needs of client goups are real, and that the level of quality is too low. He explains that this strategy has proven very efficient in the HW committee. His own experience of the politicians' reaction was that they "were paralyzed by emotions."

According to this subdepartment leader, this strategy is also a response to the worldview and policies of those whom he chose to label "the economists in the Town Hall." They "look at where they may make cutbacks, but they refuse to decide to reduce the level of municipal services." In other words, according to his view *their* problem becomes *his* dilemma. His sector is by far the most important in the municipality in terms of resources spent, and when the word "crisis" is heard, this is the place where it is supposed to occur. Because of the growing number of older, more dependent, and frail elderly in the municipality, as well as rapidly rising quality standards imposed by the central state, the demands to which his department is expected to respond are very hard to delineate. Although politicians want to reach everyone in need, at the same time they demand that the costs must be kept down. Maintaining existing service standards requires much more than the disposable resources. In general, he experiences that his own daily work is characterized by ever more ad hoc solutions. His own explanation to this problem is that "We don't have the capacity to keep ahead." He adds that he is generally very frustrated that neither politicians nor the administrative leadership seem very interested in prioritizing; they tend to leave this challenge to him, his colleagues, and the service providers.

Further down the hierarchy, dilemmas and frustrations seem to increase along the same dimensions. Many employees in the HW sector struggle with a feeling of uncertainty concerning the official status of their experience as service providers. They are supposed to provide information concerning the situation at the level of service provision, and monitor municipal performance. On the other hand they increasingly feel that when they do provide such information, their loyalty tends to be made an issue and cast in doubt. Lower-level employees are thus faced with the consequences of welfare policies in more complex ways than are their superiors. Because the discrepancy between the "is" and the "ought" has no collective, moral, or political language, they seem to be left with two uneasy possibilities: either to ignore the discrepancy by reference to loyalty and buy into the quest for organizational control, or to try to voice their uneasiness and risk sanctions.

One of the youngest welfare workers in Skien had recently started to systematize her experiences when we talked about her thoughts concerning her job in 1993. Her overall description of this experience was formulated in the following terms.

> We keep people alive, in a way....You're supposed to say 'no' and control (the costs and the clients) at the same time as you 're supposed to be a helper. That's a hell of a difficult job.

The control function is made an important part of her job: first, because the client is supposed to demonstrate the legitimacy of his or her needs, and second, because the municipality has lowered the standards of payments and insists that this is to be enforced through control of both the social worker and the client. She indicates that her own and other colleagues' reaction to this is not to care about the budgets at all, and instead provide assistance to clients that seem generally in accordance with the intention of the law. "There is oftentimes a contradictory relationship between those who have the overall responsibility on the one hand and the daily work on the other," she says. Her own solution to the loyalty problem is, as she puts it, "to put priority on *ethics* at the cost of loyalty." Presumably this was her guiding principle when she, largely backstage, played a leading part in the collective sabotage of the administrative reform in the welfare department discussed earlier in this chapter.

Among other welfare workers, the feeling of frustration is formulated in more radical terms. A basic characteristic of the experiences that give rise to ambiguity seems to be that they don't merely lead to some kind of professional resignation. The structural pressure these workers encounter also affects their identities. One says,

> I get a feeling that the employees aren't a resource for the municipalty. We who work in the Welfare Office are seen as an expenditure only, and that's quite a burden.

Like many others, he sees leadership as an indication of an increasing distance in the organization. "There's a tendency that they (leaders) seek weak, loyal leaders in the municipality," he says.

As indicated, many social workers feel strongly that they would like to, and ought to, do something about the organizational culture that leads to the construction of themselves as primarily a loyalty problem. Several of them emphasize that they ought to be more on the offensive but explain at the same time that in the long term it's almost impossible to achieve significant results. It's too exhausting to be worth it. Most seem to agree that everything stems from the lack of responsibility among the politicians. According to one of the harshest critics in the welfare department in Skien,

> Among local politicians there are many who avoid responsibility and who practice double standards. … They're partly cowardly, ignorant and unprecise. … They're only interested in what we're doing because of the money.

The main problem, he insists, is that when it comes to the test, responsibility is fragmented and the consequences are loaded upon him and his collegues.

This line of reasoning was pursued further on another occasion when I interviewed him (let us call him "H" and a colleague "B") some months later. The two agreed that the needs of the welfare clients and those working to fulfill their rights, the welfare workers, are ignored because the politicians have chosen to close their eyes and instead rely on moralism. "They don't want to see it," because "too few of them feel concretely what the problem really is." His colleague went further and said rather angrily that

> Now the politicians can avoid seeing the shit. It's we who work out in the districts who have to take it. … They don't have to take a stand, and they're experts in saying that 'We would like to change things, but our economy is too bad.' The budget always comes first.

"H" followed this up by saying that

> The discussion of values is completely absent. What do[es] the Labour Party think about how people in Skien live?. … The question concerns what ideology is. They're probably most concerned with what their calculator tells them about ideology.

When I left the office after having had lunch with the employees, "B" turned to me and said: "Now you have gotten into a rotten system." Later, when I met "B" again, he had taken another job at a local old people's home. He liked this much better. He found that working with elderly people involved much less suspicion from the politicians and others in superior positions. Moreover, he experienced that the job involved much more independence, less control from above and less stress. The elderly are very different from welfare clients, he thought, because no one doubts that their needs are natural and therefore worth responding to.

Many of the experiences that have been revealed here by welfare workers and others in the municipality in Skien are summarized in a somewhat more analytical manner by one of the representatives who participated in both the BB-project as well as in the rebellion against the reform in 1994. She starts her analysis by referring to the various "strategies for survival" that she and her colleagues develop in order to maintain some degree of motivation in their work. The main factors, she says, are "pragmatism" and "resignation." "It's a bit scary what we're willing to accept," she explains and continues by pointing out that she and her colleagues seem to be taking recourse to a different language than their own. It is the language of pragmatism; a language that "evaluates everything in economic terms," and which—strangely enough, she points out—is officially "dead" but which "has never been stronger than right now." This leaves the welfare worker with the following problem:

> Standing with one foot on the side of the law and with the other on the side of budget balance.

It places her and her collegues "in a system which distinguishes between the worthy and the unworthy," at the same time that they are supposed to disregard this dominating but largely unofficial morality. Yet it's possible, she admits, because "We're so disciplined." Then she tries to explain why there's no longer any language by which one may formulate ideas relating to conscience, dignity, and dilemma. Slightly optimistically, she identifies a kind of solution:

> Perhaps we should develop rituals by means of which we may handle the dilemmas instead of eliminating them?

When I met her about a year later, she told me that as a result of the frustration among the social workers over recent reform failures, they had begun to concentrate more intensively on developing professional work methods instead of concerning themselves with organizational matters. She presented this as a form of organizational withdrawal.

Conclusions: On Power and Autonomy

Illegal aliens in the United States, as described by Kearney, are divided personalities, split by the power of the US state apparatus´ privilege to define the relationship of self to the Other. The state exercises its power on the basis of autonomy vis-à-vis the illegal alien, who does not dare to see himself as a proper worker and citizen who may stand up and demand his rights. According to Sennet (1980), this is a typical consequence of the modern combination of power and the form of authority that arises from the ideal of autonomous leadership. With reference to ordinary work situations, he claims that workers are afraid to challenge their bosses because they think of themselves as bits and pieces of human beings who are not whole enough to be strong. (ibid., 91)

In the form of autonomous leadership, power seems to appear to be a neutral medium through which leaders are allowed to exercise influence while keeping an arm's length distance to one's subordinates and the dilemmas they face. This chapter shows how the search for autonomy, particularly among leading bureaucrats and politicians, contributes to the alienation of municipal street-level bureaucrats. Yet, it has also been shown that at the street level, employees are neither unable to articulate their experiences in alternative terms or find ways to circumvent administrative authority and orthodoxy. This seems to provide them with a repertoire of alternative interpretations and paths of action that, when the administrative authority they face is seen as poorly embedded in the institutional landscape (e.g., when it seems to lack solid political backing) may penetrate and in part undermine it, at least on a situational basis. Their ability to seek alliances that cross hierarchical levels and institutional boundaries (especially those formally separating politics and the wider civil society from the municipal bureaucracy) is vital for such purposes, and my impression is that it is well cultivated, valued, and quite widely shared. They are in no sense prisoners of the boundaries that are established as means for controlling the institution in which they work, and by means of which the institutional leadership attempts to appropriate their loyalty (and labor) and divorce it from any wider professional and ethical commitments they may have.

REFERENCES

Berger, Peter L., and Thomas Luckmann. 1967. *The Social Construction of Knowledge: A Treatise in the Sociology of Knowledge.* London: Penguin Books.

Brunsson, Nils. 1989. *The Organization of Hypocrisy: Talk, Decisions, and Action in Organizations.* New York: Wiley.

Brunsson, Nils, and Johan P. Olsen. 1993. *The Reforming Organization.* New York: Routledge.

Deetz, Stanley. 1992. *Democracy in an Age of Corporate Colonization. Developments in Communication and the Politics of Everyday Life.* Albany: State University of New York Press.

Du Gay, Paul. 2000. *In Praise of Bureaucracy: Weber, Organization, Ethics.* London: Sage.

Fukuyama, F. 2011. *The Origin of Political Order: From Prehuman Times to the French Revolution.* New York: Farrar, Strauss and Giroux.

Fukuyama, Francis. 2014. *Political Order and Political Decay: From the Industrial Revolution to the Globalisation of Democracy.* London: Profile Books.

Heyman, Josiah. 1995. Putting power in the anthropology of bureaucracy: The immigration and naturalization service at the Mexico-United States border. *Current Anthropology*, 36 (2): 261–287.

Kapferer, Bruce, and Bjørn E. Bertelsen. 2009. Introduction: The Crisis of Power and Reformations of the State in Globalizing Realities. In *Crisis of the State: War and Social Upheaval*, ed. Bruce Kapferer and Bjørn E. Bertelsen. New York: Berghahn Books.

Kearney, Michael. 1991. Borders and Boundaries of State and Self at the End of Empire. *Journal of Historical Sociology* 4 (1): 52–74.

Kronenfeld, David B., and Halvard Vike. 2002. Collective Representations and Social Praxis: Local Politics in the Norwegian Welfare State. *The Journal of the Royal Anthropological Institute* 8 (4): 621–643.

Kumlin, Staffan. 2004. *The Personal and the Political: How the Personal Welfare State Experiences Affect Political Trust and Ideology.* New York: Palgrave MacMillan.

Rothstein, Bo. 2011. *The Quality of Government: Corruption, Social Trust, and Inequality in International Perspective.* Chicago: University of Chicago Press.

Skocpol, Theda. 1992. *Protecting Soldiers and Mothers. The Origins of Social Policy in the United States.* Cambridge, Mass: Belknap.

Vike, Halvard. 1996. *Conquering the Unreal: Politics and Bureaucracy in a Norwegian Town.* Phd. thesis, University of Oslo: Department of Social Anthropology.

CHAPTER 7

The Welfare Municipality: Universalism, Gender, and Service Provision

EXCEPTIONALISM IN STREET-LEVEL BUREAUCRACY

In Scandinavia, the public sector is perhaps best characterized not by its size, but rather by its decentralized service provision system (Nagel 1991; Aronsson 1997; Arter 2008). This system is also highly personnel intensive and heavily dominated by female labor. Thus, understanding gender relations is integral to the understanding of the welfare state as such. The service-providing, overwhelmingly female labor force has adapted to the labor market in ways that are very different from what has been considered "normal" among men. In public service provision, it has proven extremely difficult for the unions to influence and regulate the relationship between available resources (personnel, competence) and service demand (Vike, Debesay and Haukelien 2016). From an employer's point of view, increasing demand and more responsibility is not necessarily a big challenge, as the service providers are used to absorbing it if they must. As a result, increasingly the labor force and the unions representing the workers are squeezed. This great adaptability and ability to deal with increasing demands for services has made service provision highly flexible, but has put service quality at great risk, and processes of "de-skilling" are clearly taking place. It seems that the welfare state has made itself structurally dependent on the reinforcement of "traditional" female adaptations to the labor market, thus reproducing

© The Author(s) 2018
H. Vike, *Politics and Bureaucracy in the Norwegian Welfare State,*
Approaches to Social Inequality and Difference,
https://doi.org/10.1007/978-3-319-64137-9_7

conventional gendered ideas of reproductively oriented work tasks as something that are most natural for women. Scandinavia is well known for its relative gender equality, which in this light appears paradoxical. In my view this paradox is rarely given the attention it deserves. In this chapter, I demonstrate how the central state and the municipalities utilize this resource, how its uses are negotiated, and how the gradual appropriation of municipal and professional autonomy by the central state influences service quality and, in the long run, seems to undermine universalism.

In Michael Lipsky's classic *Street-Level Bureaucracy* (1980) the performance of public bureaucracy is analyzed from below. In his observations of the daily work of street-level bureaucrats Lipsky reveals that they almost invariably find themselves in a dilemma. The structural conditions under which they work often contradict the policies they are to implement, both in terms of rule application, adaptation to individual needs, role combinations (service and control), and, perhaps most fundamentally, capacity. Consequently, the choices they make as they try to unite widely different social and institutional realities become acutely political. When pressured from above to produce results that can be used as political and managerial capital (winning elections, making careers), they may need to focus more on making their work look good on paper than on their actual tasks. In order to cope with the capacity problem, the professional discretion they apply may not only involve adapting policy to the individual case, and meeting real needs in the population, but often preventing patients, clients, students, or users from gaining access because the services they need, in the pragmatic gaze of the service providers, are too costly and too demanding. Because they often lack capacity to meet the demand, they must find pragmatic ways to prioritize. This is why the autonomy of the street-level bureaucracy always seems to become a key issue in institutional governance and policy implementation.

Lipsky's analysis is intriguing, as are its possible implications. Lipsky himself did not establish a comparative framework for his study, which is regrettable given its potential. As I see it, one rather obvious analytical possibility emerging from his important work involves looking more closely at how the relative autonomy of the street-level bureaucracy is in fact utilized. For example, Lipsky's subtle analysis, based on empirical material from the United States, seems strikingly relevant to the Scandinavian welfare state in this regard. In Norway, the street-level bureaucracy is not a marginal part of the state, but serves as the main interface between "the state" and the population. The Scandinavian welfare states are among the most service-intense states in the Western world, and the personnel working directly with patients, students, clients, and so on play a major role in this interface (Papakostas 2001; Vike et al. 2002). Since the 1960s in particular, the amount of services and their scope has expanded more or less continuously, and there is reason to believe that they have quite strongly influenced how the population imagine "the state" (Haukelien et al. 2011). Moreover, until quite recently, with the introduction of firmer administrative control through a massive enforcement of auditing, and of personal loyalty in the hierarchical administrative chains of command, the expansion seems to have given street-level bureaucrats a high degree of autonomy and space for maneuvering (Christensen and Lægreid 2003). The possibility of enjoying a relatively high degree of discretionary freedom seems to have been significant, as their mandate has been shaped and continually broadened, much inspired by the exceptionally optimistic welfare policies pursued by governments of all colors. As I have pointed out in previous chapters, the principle of universalism seems to have had a key role to play in reinforcing this peculiar optimism, service intensity, and the decentralized nature of the public sector. Until quite recently, the emphasis on seeking needs to meet has been far more important than guarding institutional boundaries in order to protect limited resources. Thus, the role of the street-level bureaucracy as a key interface between the state and the population is hard to overestimate (Sainsbury 1999). Because of this, it may be fruitful to ask: how exactly is the street-level bureaucracy socially embedded in this interface between the bureaucratic inside and its outside, and what are the implications? This question did not concern Lipsky. As a matter of fact, it is not often asked in studies of bureaucracy either (Rothstein 1998, 2011).

The overwhelming majority of street-level bureaucrats carry out their work as municipal employees. As has been noted by several Nordic historians and political scientists (Baldersheim et al. 1987; Nagel 1991; Aronsson 1997; Stenius 2010), the Nordic system of government could be described as a collection of *welfare municipalities*. Historically, most of what has become associated with the welfare state, the types of services and the principles guiding their provisioning, emerged first as local experiments, often initiated by voluntary associations, later institutionalized as municipal arrangements, and finally becoming a state responsibility. Today municipalities implement policy goals formulated and overseen by the central state as well as, to a large extent, financed by it. This very localized nature of the welfare state has contributed to the effect that when expressing their views on welfare state performance in the area of service provision, people tend to refer to the municipality in which they live (Haukelien et al. 2011). The overwhelming majority of street-level bureaucrats work in institutional environments where social networks are dense and overlapping enough to produce strong informal norms that actually cross the boundaries between the municipal organization and its environment. Consequently, public trust is not only, or primarily, a question of trust in government or the state, but also one of informal control within overlapping networks within the context of municipal worlds (Vike 2004; Tilly 2005).

Utopian and Contemporary Time

In this chapter I argue that the enlightened modernist vision of welfare policy involving the municipalization of responsibility are gradually being replaced by centralizing managerial visions and techniques of goal realization and control that transform the institutional conditions that made the welfare state experiment possible in the first place. The decentralization of responsibility continues, but the conditions under which local institutions assume responsibility are being radically changed. The "modernist version" of welfare policy is here taken to mean, in general terms, a system of planning, policy development, and implementation that involves negotiation at all or most levels (Friedmann 1987). By "negotiation" I refer to the organizational and communicative space necessary for securing support and legitimacy, and, not least, to be able to learn from previous mistakes and incorporate the real-world experience of those responsible for translating ideas into practice. Centralizing managerial visions, largely inspired by New Public Management philosophy tend to emphasize efficiency, loyalty, and control, and privilege the function of "the principal" (the government, the ministries, and bureaucratic managers), who make orders and in that way secure the deliveries.

This, I argue, is especially evident in the ongoing temporal shift in the conceptualization of policy: the transformation of what I call *utopian time*, or gaze, if you will, into *contemporary time* (Vike 2013). This conceptual distinction is inspired by sociologist Michael Pusey (1998: 56 ff.), who in a critique of what he sees as an "attack" on civil society in Australia speaks about "the shift in the modality of time from public time to market time," which "is experienced as the shrinking horizon of meaningfully anticipated futures." Whereas the former allows for the anticipation of the future based on what is experienced as meaningful here and now, the latter tends to come at us as a set of functional requirements to which we need to adapt. Pusey explores a number of interesting implications of this shift, the most important of which concerns trust. Drawing on Niklas Luhman, he emphasizes that reformers (in the market and in the public sector) tend to treat trust as something that "is only required if a bad outcome would make you regret your action" (ibid., 58). I find Pusey's perspective highly fruitful, and for the purpose of throwing light on my own observations I have chosen to adapt it. In my own conceptualization, utopian time is to be seen as the horizon of the possible, a temporal framework within which a collective movement along a path approaches a set of goals, goals that motivate, provide hope, and as a consequence tend to make people willing to sacrifice something on the way. Most important, in my perspective, is that utopian time may instill a degree of patience (services that aren't available now will probably be available soon), and at the same time (at least ideally) a mutual obligation on the part of the interests that have achieved the compromises necessary to establish it. Such obligations, for instance, of the kind that prevent strikes, sabotage, resignation, institutional fragmentation, and the like, are predicated on trust and may generate more of it. Contemporary time, on the other hand, is the temporal mode of the market transaction, that is, the logic of immediate return. In policy terms, it involves the replacement of a policy goal involving shared responsibility between the involved actors by a set standard, or guarantee (most often in the form of citizen rights) defined by the state. Contemporary time is equivalent to "utopia now." In Norwegian politics, contemporary time is the temporal horizon within which universal welfare becomes individual rights guaranteed by the state, to be fulfilled here and now, not by the central state by the municipalities. As I show, this transformation has massive implications, and it mirrors a major centralization of welfare politics in Norwegian society. The structural dilemma inherent in this is that individual welfare guarantees—more services and better quality for more people for less money—give rise to a major overload problem on the part of the public sector. Although the overload problem as such is not new, "utopia now" definitely is. The pressure put upon service-providing institutions and professions to operate within the horizon of contemporary time means, in principle, that power and responsibility are being strictly separated. The representatives of the central state largely perform utopian time as they reserve for themselves the privilege to push their responsibility for the capacity problem to budgetary issues that are to be dealt with sometime in the future.

I believe that elder care provides interesting illustrations of this transformation and its implications. The most important element in this, it seems to me, is the specialization of political and administrative functions and the attribution of differentiated temporality to these functions. The central state specializes in setting the standards for public services, and "orders" (or outsources) them. Then it establishes regimes of auditing, which serve as a mechanism for controlling whether the standards are met. By doing this, it transforms politics into administration and an institutional hierarchy of command. Most fundamentally, perhaps, it creates wholly new possibilities for sewing a direct link of solidarity between state political elites and the individual service recipient, reinforcing the image of "the bureaucracy," inefficient municipalities, and the self-interest of the service-providing professions that are the default causes of insufficient, inaccessible, or low-quality services.

Among the key dimensions in the comparative study of Western welfare states, the relationship among the state, the individual, and the family stands out as one of major importance. As Gösta Esping-Andersen and other comparative sociologists have shown, the continental and South European welfare state model, for instance, differs in several ways from the Scandinavian version as it rests heavily on the ability of families to take responsibility for children and the elderly (Esping-Andersen 1990, 2002). The Scandinavian model is generally seen as an institutional order that significantly reduces individuals' dependence on their families. Another relevant dimension is, as discussed earlier in this book, welfare state universalism. The British and the North American versions are often characterized as provisional, resting heavily on the testing of the legitimacy of clients' needs. These differences and their entailments have been thoroughly discussed in many contexts. Political scientists have discussed them with reference to political legitimacy, fiscal challenges, and democratic decline among others; management theorists have concerned themselves with organizational efficiency and with administrative responses to political decision making; whereas comparative sociologists have focused on much broader issues of political economy and on issues of class and social marginalization. However, some major issues have been more or less left out of the picture. How is universalism possible, and what characterizes its organizational dynamics?

Many theorists of globalization have pointed out that overload problems constitute the major challenge for all modern states, and that these problems serve as the platform for neoliberalism and the retrenchment of European welfare states (Glyn 2006; Kapferer and Bertelsen 2010; Greve 2012). In this light, it is interesting to note that there do not yet seem to be strong indications that Scandinavian states have responded by actually reducing their emphasis on universalism and the rather massive implications in terms of state responsibility entailed by this principle. One possible, and in my mind very interesting, reason for this may be related to the very fact that the welfare state's ability to maximize individual autonomy has freed women to enter the public sector as specialists in highly labor-intensive and extremely flexible care-oriented tasks. As pointed out above, the welfare state rests very heavily on female labor, which completely dominates in the welfare services and in primary education. The intimate relationship between state-driven individualization and female labor has contributed strongly to making the public sector flexible, extremely accessible, and thus fundamentally "open." In contrast to most other "normal" organizations, public service-delivering organizations in the Nordic countries, such as municipalities and hospitals, can be characterized by their fundamental lack of boundary-maintaining mechanisms. They have very little real control over the amount of work and responsibility delegated to them. Thus, for grassroots bureaucrats, overwhelming responsibility and problems of capacity tend to become personal dilemmas. "The problem of women" emerges in policy discourse as a question of why sick leave rates are high and efficiency is low.

No Man's Land

During the last decade a group of colleagues and I have studied the consequences of state policies at the local municipal level as they affect identities, discourses, and service provision. Given the Norwegian overall ambition to provide more universal welfare for less money, the institutional problem becomes how and where to draw boundaries: how to cut costs, delimit services, and control service providers without touching the ambition to achieve more, and at the same time reinforce universalism as the paramount policy principle. Women in the caring professions continually experience that the amount of work increases, that cutbacks in resources are made regularly, that they have to run faster, that the time available to coordinate services and update themselves professionally diminishes, and that leaders expect them to be more creative. As a result, they make illegitimate political priorities on a daily basis, a responsibility they tend to assume as part of their own identity work. They concentrate on the most needy patients only, ignore certain time-consuming procedures, spend less time on coordination and less time with patients, focus on tasks that have short-term effects, and, generally, work overtime more or less for free in order to get the work done and secure minimum quality. Because their responsibility for patients and clients is so personal, they not only tend to internalize organizational insufficiency as bad conscience, but their efforts contribute to modifying and hiding the effects of state and municipal welfare policy.

Much evidence suggests that the only pragmatic solution to the capacity problem available to the municipalities is to establish some kind of boundary that may reduce the overwhelming demand for costly welfare services. This involves, at least in part, manipulating quality standards as well as the actual quality of the services themselves. At the level of local politics, doing this openly is not yet really seen as an option, but it can quite easily be done indirectly through "value for money reforms." Such reforms normally involve less time per user, more users per service provider, and less coordination of services combined with ambitious quality goals and intentions. By establishing a double-bind situation among the service providers, they involve making the female workforce work much more, thus relying upon personalized responsibility towards clients, especially in elder care services.

Unlike, for example, medical doctors, elder care service providers have a difficult time legitimizing their capacity problem and its implication for quality. In formal terms, the only available way to objectify it is though "deviance reports," reporting in minute detail, for each individual case, how they fail to perform their jobs according to set standards. All available evidence suggests that, apart from being a fundamentally unattractive option because it is impractical and humiliating, it is rarely taken seriously by administrative leaders simply because the implications are too costly. As these types of welfare services become ever more financially burdensome, the central state and municipal authorities alike seem increasingly to deal with them not as competence intensive, but only as labor intensive. Thus in elder care in particular, a process of proletarization is clearly taking place. Unskilled workers are increasingly hired in nonpermanent, part-time jobs, and thus the workforce becomes seriously fragmented. Behind this a pragmatic, strongly gender-biased rationality is developing: professional competence is seen as a luxury because, after all, care for the elderly is seen as the natural capacity of any woman. Moreover, the labor force in this sector is notoriously perceived as "inefficient," female employees are "known to complain a lot," their professional standards are often considered completely unrealistic, and they are more often ill and on sick leave than the "normal" workforce.

In Norway, women constitute between 80 and 90% of the workforce in municipal health and welfare services, and in primary education the share is almost equally high. As Norwegian nursing scholar, Runar Bakken, has pointed out, these services constitute a "no man's land" (2004). The extremely gendered nature of the labor market in general, and in the public sector in particular, has some dramatic consequences and concerns the political economy of the welfare state in fundamental ways. Despite its great potential as a source of labor union power, the workforce is highly fragmented and contrasts very strongly with male-dominated unions, both those associated with the social democratic labor movement, and profession-based ones, such as the Norwegian Union of Medical Doctors. Although nurses have in fact been able to achieve some degree of monopoly over some specific medical tasks that require competence of a kind close to that of medical doctors, most tasks can, in principle, be carried out by anyone. The Norwegian Nurses' Union has never been part of the labor movement, and has been reluctant to join forces with the Union of Nurse Assistants, which is part of the social democratic labor movement. Because of the lack of union pressure, it has not been necessary for governments to specify the competence needed to perform tasks or specific quality standards, or define quantitative personnel requirements. Because of the shifting and unpredictable nature of the type and amount of needs in the population, the female workforce is responsible for responding to them regardless of their capacity or competence. The relational nature of the services they provide, moreover, enables employers to utilize what we may call the moral economy of bad conscience. Responsibility is highly individualized, and workers are exposed to a heavy pressure not to voice concerns over the quality of the services they are able to provide. In our own research in the sector, we have observed a strong tendency to the effect that voicing such concerns triggers managerial responses insisting that quality primarily depends on individual efforts; it is always possible to point to someone who is able to cope better and do a more satisfactory job.

Having observed municipal service provision through an anthropological lens over a period of twenty years, I also see another pattern emerging. Until relatively recently, around the turn of the century, workers would not be very hesitant in expressing their concerns and frustration that the responsibility they were given was in no way matched with necessary resources. The implication of this mismatch, they pointed out, was that many people in need were indeed given inadequate services. This observation, they believed, would make politicians, managers, and the wider public aware of a problem that had to be solved. Their sense of being important "witnesses," due to their direct experiences with users, often encouraged them to speak out even in public, optimistically assuming that increasing knowledge among decision makers about what is really going on was the main problem. When providing such information on municipal arenas or to the public, workers would most often experience much and intense support.

Their case was, and partly still seems to be, a morally strong one, and this contributes to throwing light on the strength and depth of support for public welfare services in Norwegian municipalities. This discourse, and its implications, is framed in the temporal context of utopian time. In media coverage on such issues, when workers "reveal" problems related to inadequate services, they almost invariably trigger a "scandal," mobilizing a discourse of scepticism concerning the real commitments among politicians and managers to do what is expected of them. Other related questions, such as the responsibility taken or not taken by next of kin, does not seem to have a legitimate place in this discourse. This, to me, indicates that in municipal worlds, the moral status of the universalist approach to the welfare state is indeed strong. Indeed, it seems that there is a widespread belief by the public that the universalist ambition constitutes an index of a moral quality, and that it is possible, although perhaps not reached as of yet. Utopian goals are simultaneously present and absent. They are, it is hoped, to be realized in the future, and in the meantime, the logical thing to do is to join forces to achieve them and negotiate the terms. In the political language of the welfare state, the conventional way to talk about political responsibility in the domain of welfare services and education is to emphasize that it amounts to a process if improvement is geared to the future. Although governments, regardless of political color, will emphasize that resources may still be more or less inadequate in relation to many political ambitions, the temporal disjunction does not present itself as a logical or practical barrier to the practice of granting utopian goals as concrete rights to services. As a result, not being able to meet the needs emerging from rights granted is not really a political challenge, but an exclusive responsibility on the part of the municipalities and the female workforce.

This temporal disjunction seems to facilitate a process I choose to call *the decentralization of dilemma*. Political responsibility is future oriented, but service provision is here and now. Their asymmetrical relation makes it logically impossible to make claims based on problems arising in contemporary time. The terms dictating the world of contemporary time are set by actors who themselves are accountable to what they intend to do in the near future. It would appear that such a logic would rapidly break down under the pressure of lack of trust. But a striking feature of the political culture of the Norwegian welfare state is exactly that political optimism still looms large. Imagining the political community as a common good and acting *as if* the welfare state is capable of and will actually deliver, seems to rest on a powerful set of beliefs with wide-ranging implications.

SERVICE PROVISION AND CONTEMPORARY TIME

Many service providers (nurses and assistant nurses) explain that they experience an overwhelming scarcity of resources. They are unable to meet their responsibilities, and when confronting their leaders they are told that they have to try to cope the best they can. "We simply lack the money," their leaders often complain. Therefore, they need to try to find ways to increase efficiency and "cut corners," for example, by spending less time on each patient or simply running faster. Other strategies may involve trying to prevent patients from returning early to the hospital, ignoring some patients during weekends, and letting unskilled staff take responsibility for medicine distribution and other tasks that formally speaking require particular qualifications.

> Very often I see that there is no way I can meet the client's needs, because I lack the time.

> The patients I treat are very sick – terminal patients in the elderly home, and some living at home who are so needy that when I come to visit their

next of kin "escape" in order to get some time off. The staff is exhausted, and then we need to hire more unskilled substitutes.

> When there's no more money and it is impossible to find substitutes, I have to call next of kin and tell them that "Sorry, we will not be able to do the job the coming weekend." That is quite exhausting.

According to many informants, sick leave tends increasingly to be used by the staff strategically as a means to recover. Many refer to "burnout."

> No one really knows about the situation we're in. … [If] I get sick I know that there's a fair chance that no one will be able to take over the responsibility, and I have to personally recruit substitutes. Every time I try to present our problems to the leaders, I'm told that I am maximizing crisis.

A main problem, as most of the female workforce sees it, is that no one seems willing to acknowledge the problems they face, and that they lack recognition.

> I never hear anything from my superiors, regardless of what I do. Even when things get really fucked up, you don't hear anything. They simply stay away and keep the distance.

When they voice their concerns, they feel that it quickly turns into questions of loyalty. It tends to be interpreted as an attempt to portray the municipality in "negative" terms that create an "unfavorable picture" of the state of affairs. They then appear as employees who sabotage the attempt to cultivate positive attitudes and the portrayal of an "attractive" municipality.

> I feel that I am really loyal to the organization, but sometimes I have to be "disloyal" in the sense that I hire extra staff in order to cope and use too much money – to call an elderly client who is physically very weak and tell her that she won't get any help from us in the weekend, that's tough. When I get very tired I can't stand making these calls any longer, and then I don't give a damn and instead I hire extra people.

The mutual suspicion that has developed between different hierarchical levels in the municipal organization has contributed to a form of interaction characterized by a muted dialogue about things that have become illegitimate to talk about openly. As the staff experiences it, this threatens their sense of dignity and makes them feel that they are constantly being seen as disloyal. Consequently, they need to demonstrate the opposite, and that they are indeed moral persons. This need also arises from the fact that leaders are frustrated that employees complain too much, and are negative. Thus, they see a need to implement measures that can improve the work environment, or "work culture."

The employees feel that their effort to prevent the municipal capacity problem from turning into a full-blown crisis by circumventing rules, cutting corners, running faster, and so on, is what really keeps the municipal organization and its reputation afloat. The irony here is that when state authorities audit municipal services and identify instances of deviation, those who set the goals and cut down on resources are not subject to scrutiny, only those who carry the responsibility and work under conditions they have no means to influence are.

> It's like pissing in one's pants to keep warm. For [a] while I considered re-classifying clients who qualified for immediate assistance so that they could be put on the waiting list, but it's an illusion to think that that solves the problem; after a short while you get the heart-breaking situations and you have to leave everything and attend to it immediately.

> ..., but all the things I do in my office – that which may determine the future trajectory of client cases – somehow become less important – what matters is to make many decisions in one day. All the other work I do, the really important work, is what makes me lag seriously behind.

> I spend four or five hours per week trying to comfort and support next of kin whose frail elderly kin do not get sufficient municipal care. I have never before experienced so much frustration and aggression among next of kin as now. I have almost become afraid of answering the phone; I kind of jump in my chair when it rings.

The experiences of street-level bureaucrats in Norwegian municipalities reported here can be interpreted in several different ways. One common comment among managers, politicians, part of the wider public, and many scholars, is that people in these services tend to complain a lot. One aspect of this is the opinion that "there will never be enough resources," and the discrepancy between goals and resources has always existed and probably always will. This may be part of the reason why in political debate, administrative discourse, and scholarly analysis it is represented as a problem of institutional governance and efficiency, rather than as a symptom of a structural problem.

MORE FOR LESS: THE REFORMING STATE

In 2012 the red–green Norwegian government launched a reform called *Samhandlingsreformen, The Cooperation Reform*, with broad support from the National Assembly. The purpose was to improve and strengthen the links between hospitals and municipal health and care services. Hospitals, which in the Norwegian context are categorized as "second line services," are responsible for advanced medical assistance and intervention. These services are supposed to complement municipal services and "first line services," and hospitals receive the great majority of patients from them, after preliminary medical investigation. In general, all medical needs requiring a high level of competence are channeled to hospitals. In turn, patients who have "finished treatment" are sent back to municipal care to recover (or if no further treatment is considered possible, to hopefully receive palliative care. The motivation for implementing the reform was the need to prevent patients from being sent back and forth between institutions with ambiguous and partly overlapping responsibility. A particular problem was that this ambiguous and overlapping responsibility generated competition and a lack of will/ability to secure overall responsibility for patients, as hospitals and municipalities (and various professional actors) often seemed more oriented towards delimiting their own responsibilities in order to save costs. Thus through the reform the government sought to specify how responsibility for treating and caring for patients was to be distributed between these institutions. A main mechanism was to concentrate and intensify medical treatment in hospitals and make it easier for hospitals to send patients to municipal care, even in cases where patients were in need of treatment that up until the reform was implemented had been considered "medical." Therefore, hospitals could send more patients "home" more quickly than before, and focus much more sharply on the medical problem at hand, not so much on the patients' other possible needs. In this way, each patient would require less time in hospitals, and many more could be treated. The municipalities were supposed to take responsibility for the rest, and the incentive system was adapted to institutional division of labor. Hospitals were rewarded economically for treating more patients, however, municipalities were punished for not receiving them according to the set time.

The consequences soon became visible. From the point of view of hospitals, a sharp increase in efficiency was observed due to higher turn-over. The municipalities, however, received an increasing number of patients, often at short notice (and immediately before weekends), and faced medical and caring challenges on a new scale. Many of the patients were in need of much more specialized, intense, and long-term attention than before, and this became a problem relating to both capacity and competence. A few of them had been able to invest in more personnel and competence prior to the reform, but because the central state mainly saw the reform as a device to increase efficiency, financial compensation was marginal. The overwhelming majority of Norwegian municipalities ended up assuming much more responsibility than they were able to handle.

Together with two colleagues (Heidi Haukelien and Ingvild Vardeim at Telemark Research Institute) I followed this reform in some detail as its consequences emerged in 2014 and 2015 through interviews in 12 municipalities and a comprehensive ssurvey (Haukelien et al. 2015). The majority of our respondents—nurses, assistant nurses, and middle-level leaders—concluded that cooperation between the two levels had improved in several ways, particularly due to better routines. However, service providers had experienced a considerable increase in their work-loads and responsibility for treating patients with a variety of much more complicated medical needs than previously. The main challenge reported by these respondents was that they had to deal with this without any sig-nificant increase in personnel or level of competence. It appeared that the reform was mainly a mechanism for the decentralization of respon-sibility from hospitals to municipalities. Our survey revealed that more than 90% of nurses reported that the complexity of medical treatment had increased significantly, and almost 80% had experienced increasing amounts of administrative work.

Our interviews with nurses revealed that in order to cope with the new situation, municipalities have lifted the threshold for access to ser-vices. Moreover, because patients have greater and more complex medi-cal needs, services become more vulnerable as the competence and professional infrastructure needed to deal with them is nonexistent or insufficient. As a result, although the quality of service has increased in a few prioritized areas, it has generally been lowered and more uneven. For the service providers, the sense of working in the context of a more or less permanent state of emergency dominates, as does the necessity of dealing with ethical dilemmas on an individual basis and without organizational backing. One highly problematic aspect of this, according to the nurses interviewed, is the loyalty expected on their part. Municipalities rarely want to be put in a bad light in terms of service quality, and sanction nurses who warn that service quality is threatened. As noted above, in municipal health and care services, service quality systems are normally oriented towards preventing quality from deteriorating; instead they are based on personnel reporting and documenting each instance of possible breach of standards. In this way, reporting quality problems is personalized and tends to become translated into questions of loyalty.

While working with this material, our interest was increasingly drawn to the question of how the documentation of the failures of the reform was interpreted and dealt with by responsible authorities. The Directorate of Health reported in 2013 that it was aware that the demand for more complex and varied services had increased at the municipal level, but the implications of this were not discussed in the report. The National Association of Municipalities, KS, noted that "serious weakness in elderly care" had been documented in the form of lack of competence, inadequate language skills, inadequate organizational arrangements and lack of continuity, and poor coordination and documentation. However, although this organization (KS) is supposed to represent municipal interests, the main focus in this issue was the employer's point of view. What is needed, according to KS, is "attitudes, values and more ethical reflection."

In the following, our main findings (from this research as well as previous studies conducted by Haukelien and myself, see Haukelien 2013) are organized into two categories, which I call "ambivalence" and "double bind," respectively.

A parallel ambition in the coordination reform was to expand low threshold services in the municipalities, preferably in people's own homes, at the cost of hospitalization and institutionalization in elder homes. One of the nurses' main dilemmas, partly following from this, is related to scarcity of competence. Their users have much more complex medical needs than before, and treatments that were traditionally dealt with at the hospital, have now been decentralized. The nurses emphasize that this change has not been met by an increased focus on competence, and there is simply no way to serve all the users adequately. They also emphasize that the recent rationalization of the services has given them a series of new tasks, some of which they call "housewife tasks" and "maintenance worker tasks," respectively. Cleaning kitchens, doing the laundry, changing light bulbs, informing next of kin, and so on are for efficiency reasons added to the workload of each nurse. They describe a process of medical specialization and multiplication of work tasks that, in practice, tend to produce a generalist approach to the services. In most cases municipal authorities seem very hesitant to facilitate specialization among the female workforce, as it reduces flexibility and increases costs; our impression from discussing the issue with leaders, is that it is simply seen as unnecessary luxury, despite the fact that some municipal services in fact have become mini-hospitals. Another related problem reported by the nurses is lack of intimate knowledge of each patient, which increases insecurity and the risk of making fatal errors. Moreover, a challenge arising from the increasing multitasking is that professional routines become impossible to develop and follow; instead, because one cannot predict the size and complexity of the workload, the division of labor among staff is ad hoc and complex; medical tasks are largely performed when extra time is available. More and more tasks are taken over by unskilled personnel. Nurses say that they feel a strong pressure from the unskilled personnel as a result of the collectively felt need to cooperate in order to perform the most basic task, something that makes it morally problematic to concentrate on more specialized tasks directed at individual users.

Ambivalence

A young man needs assistance several times a day for his toilet training. In order to get to his home, the nurses have to take a ferry. Normally they try to make sure that the task is assigned to one of the nurses who live on the island. On the day we join one of the nurses on duty, who lives on the mainland, an old woman calls the alarm at two o'clock. The nurse calls back and learns that the woman has peed on herself. The young man needs to be visited at set times, the next being six o'clock. The nurse must choose whether to visit him now, and then wait on the island for the returning ferry, or call the man and tell him that he must wait until the following day. She decides to go to the island and calls the woman that she has to wait until late evening.

A nurse tells us about a former patient who is now dead, and who suffered from ALS. As the disease progressed he needed a respirator machine when he rested and slept. He got steadily weaker, and one after-noon nurse Randi was the only nurse on duty, covering both the elder home and the home-based services; another patient living in his own home was reported to be dying. The respirator patient suffered not only from ALS, but had a number of other medical problems that made treatment complex and time-consuming. That day his next of kin called Randi and told her that they had reached the conclusion to turn off the respirator machine and finally let the patient pass away. Randi knew such a situation could arise, but had not anticipated that it could hap-pen now. She called the medical doctor, who told her that she could give the patient 10 mg. morphine as she removed the mask. She informed the patient about the process (she didn't get contact with him, but assumed that he could hear her), as well as his family. She found the situation to be very difficult. One thing that concerned her was the size of the mor-phine dose, which she feared could kill the patient. She called the doc-tor one more time, and he suggested that she could give half the dose. As this process unfolded, Randi made several visits to the other dying patient, who died two days later leaving Randi with a feeling that she had not been able to attend adequately to either of the two patients.

Double Bind

Administrative leaders emphasize loyalty because they do not want to nourish a negative image of the municipality among the public. When working conditions turn to worse in the elder home, the municipal authorities have tried to forbid the staff to expose the problems. In one case the staff was ordered to not inform the users' next of kin that no sub-stitutes were hired when staff fell sick. When next of kin get frustrated and complain that nurses come too late for appointments, or not at all, their superiors insist that they are not allowed to admit that the reason is lack of personnel. As a result, the nurses feel trapped: they need to perform the workloads of two or three persons simultaneously, carry the responsibility when confronted with next of kin or frustrated users personally, and try to maintain decent quality and prevent patients' health from deteriorating as a result of not having enough time to attend to them.

Lower-level leaders in elder homes and home-based services tend to share the nurses' dilemma, but are somewhat differently positioned and experience it from another angle. They emphasize the strong growth in needs, both as a result of an increasing number of frail elderly, many of whom do not have next of kin who can contribute much (either because they live far away or are very busy), and, perhaps most important, due to the massive transferral of medical responsibility from hospitals to municipalities. One major problem for these leaders is, as indicated above, that the decentralization of responsibility for users in need of complex medical treatment has not been met by increasing resources. There has been no significant increase in staff, and no systematic program for developing or attracting competent personnel. Staff who want to attend courses and educational programs often have to pay for them personally, and there is no money for hiring extra staff in their absence. At the same time these leaders often face demands to make "necessary budget cuts" without influencing service quality. Such demands tend to come in the fall, as the Municipal Assembly makes attempts to "save the budget" and, although rarely specified, such cuts almost invariably have to be done by reducing personnel or hiring less costly labor (temporary, part-time, unskilled). For these leaders, their daily work tends to become more unpredictable, administrative, more oriented to preventing crises, and less focused on professional supervision and coordination of the staff.

In contrast to other service-providing institutions based on competence-intensive activity, such as hospitals, municipal service provision in the area of municipal health and care does not follow a path of increasing specialization, or at least only marginally so. The tendency to generalize work tasks and disconnect them from specific professional roles and competences seems much stronger. As the most skilled personnel constitute a minority in most of these services, the possibility to establish authority upon professional competence is limited and tends to be undermined by unskilled or semi-skilled personnel who very often feel that their effort to make things work is not recognized. In their eyes, in the daily routine the major problem is to keep the wheels turning and carry out the most pressing tasks in the best way possible. Spending much time with individual users who may have particular needs, for example, involves investing less in the rest. This zero-sum logic is very effective and flexible, and makes it possible to utilize labor as a general adaptable resource. For nurses, however, it may cause problems. It makes it hard to cultivate particular competence-intensive responsibilities, and very difficult to make priorities according to professional, quality-related criteria. Most of the time, the nurses are needed in the collective effort to get the most important and pressing tasks done, and specialized tasks tend to be represented as a threat to the solidarity needed to maintain this collective orientation. Insisting on the need for more competence may be difficult in this context, because in many situations it becomes another way of saying that all the hard-working nonprofessional staff who keep the ship afloat is not good enough.

In one of our fieldwork projects, we observed a controversy related to the organization of the health and welfare services, which was generally regarded as very costly (Haukelien 2013). Shift plans constitute a major issue in all institutions of this type, and tend to mobilize the structural tension between worker rights and organizational costs. Rights tend to increase rigidity and may seem as a barrier to using resources directly for service quality. In order to achieve greater efficiency and save money, individual politicians in the municipality in which we did fieldwork at the time made an initiative to propose a change in the shift plan, and successfully had it prepared for the Municipal Assembly. Realizing that the health and welfare services were capable of doing the job with one less person during weekends than during the week, one politician suggested that there may not be a need for "one extra person" between weekends. He had not considered the distribution of actual tasks and workloads between the two periods, and he did not relate to the fact that many of the tasks that staff did not have time to perform during weekends, could be done before or after. His proposal achieved a majority in the Assembly because it solved a very difficult budget problem. Our own impression was that the proposal was not seen as deeply problematic, or arrogant. Rather, it seemed us to reflect a respect for the flexibility characterizing the female workforce in this municipality. "The girls at the elderly home will certainly be able to take care of this," one administrative leader pointed out, commenting the argument that the issue should perhaps have been better prepared.

Conclusions: Utopia Now! And Its Gendered Consequences

The pattern emerging from these examples is not only that the female workforce in the welfare state represents a striking contrast to "ordinary" labor adaptations in the high-skilled labor market, but also that the services it provides seem highly accessible. For several interesting reasons the workforce seems hesitant to compensate for difficult working conditions by protecting itself from overwhelming demand. If this is a reasonable interpretation, the explanation may not be very hard to identify. Although seemingly irrational in light of what many scholars seem to deem typical among street-level bureaucrats (in the tradition of Michael Lipsky), these actors are incorporated in a tradition formed in a period of exception expansion and optimism, as well as a high degree of professional autonomy. Instead of developing strategies of protection that may secure some autonomy vis-à-vis employers and users presenting them with impossible dilemmas, they have largely chosen to adapt and to stick to the expectation that better insight in what "really" goes on will bring rewards in the future. This belief seems to become reinforced by their identification with the users and their next of kin, who regard the services they provide as important and attractive, and who generally want more of them.

It may not be a far-fetched hypothesis to assume that here lies one major foundation for the general public trust in public institutions: after all, services such as these constitute the major interface between the public and "the state" (qua municipal performance). Moreover, the moral pressure to be accessible and to deliver is nourished by the internal competition between staff, which is normally not organized in ways that facilitate horizontal solidarity across professional identities and often extremely individualized responsibilities, and which ties individual staff directly to leaders and their tastes. The coordination it would require to act more in union, for example, by demonstrating scarcity and the fatal consequences that are likely to emerge from less accessibility, is most often not seen as realistic or even desirable. Indeed, in a large number of cases we have witnessed nurses and assistant nurses who try to do this, and who tend to start with arguing that the quality of services is being undermined, are publicly confronted by colleagues who claim that "In our unit, we focus on the users and are able to deliver high quality." This type of internal competition leaves the unions with severe difficulties when trying to argue for systematic change.

In this chapter, I have introduced the metaphoric image of two interrelated temporalities: utopian and contemporary time, arguing that institutions and personnel responsible for making the elusive promises (Abram and Wezskalnys 2013) of the welfare state in fact transform a vision of the future into something very concrete here and now. State authorities deal with their political responsibility as "goals," and municipalities and service providers are legally responsible for the same goals as legally codified citizen rights. This division of labor is systematically gendered. In my interpretation, the logical and practical contradiction involved in this dual temporality is modified and at the same time partly legitimated by the flexibility of the (female) workforce. By assuming the responsibility to make priorities that are, strictly speaking, deeply political, and simultaneously cultivating a subject position that enables them to see themselves as partly "outside" the organization that employs them, they seem to be able to cope with the cognitive dissonance they experience and "solve" the practical and ethical challenges they encounter. However, there are certain fairly strong indications that the situation is changing, and that their institutional "withdrawal" does not to any significant degree involve a robust horizontally organized backstage arena in the form described on the part of the social workers in Chap. 6. It may even become increasingly individualized and privatized. Although, somewhat paradoxically, the autonomy of service providers in elder care is in some ways substantial, it is extremely difficult to transform into collective action. As I emphasized earlier in this chapter, this seems to have reinforced the impression among decision makers that "the problem of women" in these services is paramount, due to high sick leave rates, deteriorating work environments, insufficient service provision, and the like. However, as I hope to have shown in this chapter, there are some quite obvious and nonpoliticized reasons why the structural contractions of the welfare state tend to be attributed to women working as street-level bureaucrats. It may be seen as a great paradox that the relative success of a well-organized labor movement in Norway has failed to inspire the conceptualization of the female workforce in this sector in terms of class and political mobilization.

REFERENCES

Abram, Simone, and Weszkalnys (eds.). 2013. *Elusive Promises. Planning in the Contemporary World*. New York: Berghahn Books.

Aronsson, Petter. 1997. Local Politics – The Invisible Political Culture. In *The Cultural Construction of Norden*, eds. Øystein Sørensen and Bo Stråth, 172–206. Oslo: Scandinavian University Press.

Arter, David. 2008. *Scandinavian Politics Today*. Manchester: Manchester University Press.

Bakken, Runar. 2004. *Mann i ingenmannsland. Om menn i omsorg, hjemme og ute*. Bergen: Fagbokforlaget.

Baldersheim, Harald et al. 1987. *Folkestyre i by og bygd. Norske kommuner gjennom 150 år*. Oslo: Universitetsforlaget.

Christensen, Tom, and Per Lægreid. 2003. *New Public Management: The Transformation of Ideas and Practice*. Hampshire: Ashgate Publishing Limited.

Esping-Andersen, Gösta. 1990. *The Three Worlds of Welfare Capitalism*. Cambridge: Polity Press.

Esping-Andersen, Gösta. 2002. *Why We Need a New Welfare State*. Oxford: Oxford University Press.

Friedmann, John. 1987. *Planning in the Public Domain. From Knowledge to Action*. Princeton: Princeton University Press.

Glyn, Andrew. 2006. *Capitalism Unleashed. Finance, Globalization, and Welfare*. New York/Oxford: Oxford University Press.

Greve, Bent. (ed.) 2012. *The Times They are Changing. Crisis and The Welfare State*. Malden/Oxford: Wiley-Blackwell.

Haukelien, Heidi et al. 2011. *Frihet til likeverd: likhetsverdier, lokal tilpasning og ansvarsfordeling*. Report no. 281. Bø: Telemarksforsking.

Haukelien, Heidi et al. 2015. *Samhandlingsreformens konsekvenser i de kommunale helse- og velferdstjenestene. Sykepleieres erfaringer*. Report no. 362. Bø, Telemark: Telemarksforsking.

Lipsky, Michael. 1980. *Street-Level Bureaucracy. Dilemmas of the Individual in Public Services*. New York: Russel Sage Foundation.

Nagel, Anne Hilde (ed.). 1991. *Velferdskommunen. Kommunenes rolle i utviklingen av velferdsstaten*. Bergen: Alma Mater.

Papakostas, Apostolis. 2001. Why is There No Clientelism in Sweden? In *Clientelism, Interests, and Democratic Representation. The European Experience in Historical and Comparative Perspective*, ed. Simona Piattoni, 31–54. Cambridge: Cambridge University Press.

Pusey, Michael. 1998. Between Economic Dissolution and the Return to the Social: The Contest for Civil Society in Australia. In *Real Civil Societies. Dilemmas of Institutionalization*, ed. Jeffrey Alexander, 40–66. London: Sage.

Rothstein, Bo. 1998. *Just Institutions Matter. The Moral and Political Logic of the Universal Welfare State*. Cambridge: Cambridge University Press.

Rothstein, Bo. 2011. *The Quality of Government. Corruption, Social Trust, and Inequality in International Perspective*. Chicago: University of Chicago Press.

Sainsbury, Diane. 1999. *Gender and welfare state regimes*. Oxford: Oxford University Press.

Stenius, Henrik. 2010. Nordic Associational Life in a European and an Inter-Nordic Perspective. In *Nordic Associations in a European Perspective*, ed. Henrik Stenius, and Risto Alapuro. Nomos: Baden-Baden.

Tilly, Charles. 2005. *Trust and Rule*. Cambridge: Cambridge University Press.

Vike, Halvard et al. 2002. *Maktens samvittighet. Om politikk, styring og dilemmaer i velferdsstaten*. Oslo: Gyldendal.

Vike, Halvard. 2004. *Velferd uten grenser. Den norske velferdsstaten ved veiskillet*. Oslo: Akribe.

Vike, Halvard. 2013. Egalitarianisme og byråkratisk individualisme. *Norsk antropologisk tidsskrift* 24 (3–4): 181–193.

Vike, Halvard, Jonas Debesay, and Heidi Haukelien (eds.). 2016. *Tilbakeblikk på velferdsstaten. Politikk, styring og tjenester*. Oslo: Gyldendal.

CHAPTER 8

Egalitarianism and Individual Autonomy in the Northern European Periphery

Psychotherapy in Cultural Context

Assuming that there are highly significant differences among scenarios of state formation across Europe that are perhaps partly unacknowledged (Tilly 1990, 2004; Trägårdh 2008; Stenius 2010; Collins 2011), our ability to describe and explain them depends upon a systematic attention to the way in which specific social forms are institutionalized in the state. Because of this, a historically oriented anthropology of Western European state formation is needed. The Scandinavian countries constitute an interesting case in point because, here, some general dynamics in the development of Western European states were played out in a way that led to a particularly ambitious type of democratic state capitalism. One key characteristic of this type of state is that its expansive welfare policies have freed a substantial portion of the population from market dependency and personal dependency, thereby fundamentally blurring the boundaries between "the state" and civil society and generating a form of "statist individualism" that promotes a particular idea of freedom (Trägårdh 1997). This idea of freedom seems strongly associated with autonomy. It is not a classic liberal version, which is above all else about freedom from the state, but instead freedom understood as individual rights to more and better public services, which secures a material basis for not becoming dependent on others: kin, neighborhood, civil society, and, to some extent employers. My analytical interest in this particular political experiment relates to the need to explain why it—as

© The Author(s) 2018   157
H. Vike, *Politics and Bureaucracy in the Norwegian Welfare State,*
Approaches to Social Inequality and Difference,
https://doi.org/10.1007/978-3-319-64137-9_8

an otherwise "typical" European type of state—seems to have become so atypical in its approach to contemporary challenges related to social reproduction.

In 2013, together with my colleague Heidi Haukelien I carried out fieldwork in a psychotherapeutic context, Modum Psychiatric Clinic, also located in the southeast of Norway. The clinic is a publicly funded autonomous institution originally emerging from visionary humanistic psychiatry and Christian (Lutheran) voluntarism. During fieldwork, we got to know the psychotherapeutic teams, many of the patients, and followed the work as it took place in a variety of contexts, mainly therapy, psychoeducational sessions, coordinating activities, and some more informal settings. Our ambition, as anthropologists, was to try to understand how patients experienced the processes they went through during their stay at the clinic; that is, how and why they attributed meaning to the contexts they became involved in, and how they related to the affordances provided by such contexts to better understand and deal with their psychological and relational challenges. In this chapter, I explore ways in which psychotherapy draws on the wider cultural context in which it is embedded, and choose in particular to look at the idea of individual autonomy. When trying to find ways to understand and develop mental-health–promoting patterns of social interaction, therapists and patients draw on a repertoire of meanings embedded in cultural history. In the Norwegian context, individual autonomy and egalitarianism constitute important parts of this repertoire (Sørensen and Stråth 1997). In the first part of the chapter, I focus on family therapy, which, to me, serves as a particularly interesting illumination of these themes. The second part elaborates another major related theme in this book: how specific institutional contexts play an important role in assisting people in constructing worldviews.

In previous chapters, I discussed how what I call "the low level of gravity state" provides such contexts, and particularly how the municipal institution enables actors to think about universalism and develop strategies for realizing political and professional interests that seek to challenge the central state's construction of responsibility for welfare services. I pointed out that in municipal worlds, institutional boundaries have tended to be highly porous and perhaps well adapted to providing services on a universal basis. In local politics, it has been possible to build horizontal alliances and mobilize politically to try to realize this ideal. At Modum Psychiatric Clinic, institutional boundaries play a very different role. Here they serve as a device for distinguishing patients who are in fact admitted for treatment from all those who apply but must wait in queue or are rejected. This enables the institution to adjust its resources to the treatment of a set number of patients. Consequently, the concern with quality is very different from that in municipal service, and this concern is moored in a robust type of professional autonomy. I find it interesting that, presumably due to these structural conditions, professional ideals concerning policy models for psychiatric treatment take a very particular form. This, I argue, is relevant in light of the increasing tension I have discussed in previous chapters between universalism and managerial governance in municipal worlds. At Modum, the ideals concerning policy models for psychiatric treatment fit very nicely with state policy. As I show, I see this as a reflection of the particular institutional context within which these ideals are formulated, one that contrasts sharply with municipal contexts that in fact carry the bulk of the responsibility for this kind of treatment. First, however, I focus on how psychotherapy at Modum Psychiatric Clinic and its wider cultural context inspires and enables professionals and patients to imagine egalitarianism and individual autonomy in specific ways.

Dilemmas of Symmetrical Reciprocity

In *"The Pathological Family: Postwar America and the Rise of Family Therapy,"* Deborah Weinstein (2013) presents a fascinating account of the intellectual history of a very diverse psychotherapeutic tradition. One essential feature seems to be the combination of a certain intellectual openness and the complexity of its subject matter. Moreover, because of the symbolic significance of the nuclear family in the postwar and late modern Western context, particularly its role as a key arena for the reproduction of democratic values and the like, family therapy deals with much larger issues than those reducible to individual health. In the Norwegian and Scandinavian context, such issues tend to touch upon gender equality, the role of autonomy within the context of the dyadic partnership, and perhaps especially on the art of stimulating children's sense of security through experimenting with autonomy. Thus in most of the therapeutic and educational sessions we took part in during our fieldwork we encountered reflections and discussions circling around dilemmas related to balancing social and emotional obligations with individual boundaries and autonomy. Very often the key term that was introduced to mediate the tensions that grew out of this dilemma was "attachment," indicating that there may be a way to attain some harmony, or balanced reciprocity, between the exclusive bonds of the family and the autonomy of its individual members.

As they appeared to us in this therapeutic context, dilemmas of this kind clearly reflected tensions of a more structural type. As Antony Giddens (1991) and others (Berger et al. 1974; Beck 2002) have pointed out, in historical and sociological terms, late modernity presents us with some very unique challenges as to how to achieve and cultivate intimacy. According to Giddens, love and intimacy are no longer compatible with "traditional" obligations because our tolerance for personal dependence is so radically reduced. In order to be emotionally rewarding, intimacy can hardly survive if it not anchored in what he calls "pure relationships." Although of course an ideal conceptual type, "pure relationships" come close to what many people seem to value highly; they leave no other strings attached than the bonds of love themselves and keep intimacy alive by being exclusive and conditional upon nothing but itself and whatever other emotional qualities nourish it. Clearly this conceptualization of intimacy and love is highly simplifying, but for my purpose in this chapter—attempting to contextualize family therapy in the Norwegian cultural context—it does seem to have some analytical value.

In Norway and Scandinavia at large, individual autonomy carries particular salience beyond the world of middle-class men. For a number of historical reasons, but not least as a result of the social and cultural effects of the welfare state, individual dependency has become a widely shared and celebrated value. The relative success of Scandinavian feminism is a major aspect of this; the institutionalization of the historical demands for economic security and freedom from dependence on caretaking obligations is a reality for the majority. The universal nature of public services (child care and elder care in particular) and economic compensation for unemployment and the like have not only served to "naturalize" autonomy as a more or less self-evident cultural value shared by men and women alike; it has also become *partly* independent of class. Although empirically such a statement (regarding social class) is not at all in complete accord with the realities, I want to point out that in a context such as Modum Psychiatric Clinic, the discursive effects of the cultural ideas of the middle classes can hardly be exaggerated. Here, as in many other public contexts in Norwegian society, social class constitutes a "silent" category which, even though evident to most as systems of distinction available for decoding, is normally not a legitimate topic to be made relevant in social interaction. As many ethnographic accounts of Norwegian society have demonstrated, this has some profound effects (Barnes 1954; Gullestad 1992). One of them is that alternatives to the middle-class worldview tend to become muted and seen mainly as a temporary stage, as but one step on the ladder to "normality" (Löfgren 1987; Stenius 2010). Another effect is that the eagerness by which many seem to grasp the possibility to adjust to middle-class norms is considerable, and to some extent realistic, considerably more so than in societies where economic security and social status depend solely on wage labor, family status, or inheritance. Although the institutions of the welfare state have not contributed significantly to abolishing socioeconomic inequality, but have gone a very long way to universalize access to an attractive (mainly "middle-class") life style. Regardless of its many problems, there is little doubt the welfare state can be seen as an extraordinary successful achievement in sociocultural integration.

AUTONOMY AND BOUNDARIES

Couples who come to Modum Bad to seek therapeutic treatment look for ways to change relationships and emotional states. As it appeared to us during our fieldwork, they most often sought alternatives to asymmetric reciprocity. In other words they did not seem to desire complementarity vis-à-vis their partners beyond the emotional reward of love; asymmetry was tolerable only to the extent that it could be regarded as an "accidental" outcome of different and shifting preferences between equals. What they looked for was in a sense a version of themselves in their partners. I do not want to caricature egalitarian partnerships of love, but regard it necessary to emphasize that the normative and emotional prioritization of autonomy was fundamental among most patients we met at Modum. In the cultural context of Norway and the Nordic countries, which I have tried to describe in somewhat superficial terms above, this may not be very surprising.

In psychoeducational settings where the participants (partners and some single mothers) discussed norms and ideals related to emotionally rewarding relationships of love, there seemed to be full agreement that the breadwinner-based family model involving the female partner as a specialist provider of love, caretaking, and "quality time" is hopelessly out of date. Also with reference to socializing children, the conversations we took part in cultivated the egalitarian idea that enlightened parents do not, or should not, base their authority on some particular function in the family; this would potentially undermine the autonomy of each partner as well as distort their children's idea of what real equality is about. The main problem arising from these norms and insights seemed to be that "the content" of symmetrical reciprocity turned out to be quite hard to identify; it may be difficult to find out what kind of gift to provide when in principle any gift may undermine your partner's paramount value, his or her autonomy. However, the dilemma was only rarely formulated in such terms, only hinted at, and in most contexts the problem was mainly one of abstraction. The therapists' main message was that dilemmas of egalitarian reciprocity are related to the art of recognizing one's partner regardless of his or her specific achievements. The participants acknowledged this insight and worked with it in several ways, but the challenge of bringing this message down to the level of daily interaction remained a challenge for many, as we understood it.

The problem of egalitarian reciprocity as an emergent property of recognition was closely related to another key topic in family therapy at Modum Psychiatric Clinic: that of "personal boundaries." "Personal boundaries" was a much discussed theme during sessions, and the way it was made relevant always seemed to underscore its importance as a basic prerequisite for mental health and healthy relations in the family. As a therapeutic category it proved very useful, as most patients could use it to conceptualize aspects of themselves and their family relations, and at the same time acknowledge it as a widely shared normative standard. Its scope of applicability was broad; we first encountered it in the form of a therapeutic warning to the patients as a group. They were reminded that they should tell their personal stories to others with some care, taking into consideration that being given more information about the problems of others may cause distress rather than enabling listeners as partners in productive conversations. Later we learned about it in the form of a theory of self-empowerment, which was frequently communicated in psychoeducative settings. The basic idea was that the ability to receive the acknowledgment of others and use it for strengthening one's self-esteem, depends on not being in a state of "leaking." Low self-esteem tends to generate a hunger for recognition, but the recognition offered cannot do the job of building self-esteem because it always "leaks out" in greater quantities than any "refill" can match. A third important version of the personal boundary theme was about not being able to care sufficiently about one's own needs, and instead become too concerned with the needs of others. Not being able to say "no" was one typical formulation of this problem.

The challenge of building and guarding personal boundaries typically became a red thread in the couples therapy sessions we observed during our fieldwork, and, perhaps needless to say, at a much higher level of complexity. The typical case would be difficult communicative situations in which the therapist(s) and one of the key actors together would try to communicate to the other actor that he or she is about to break the boundaries of integrity in some specific way. Such attempts would, as we experienced them, often fail and would need to be repeated if necessary in later sessions, in combination with other strategies through which the same point could be brought forth and maybe across. Such attempts seemed to us as "moments of truth" in the sense that further progress depended upon "the object" becoming visible and made into a problem of reflection as something "outside" the actors' identities. The contrast between partner egalitarianism as an "ideological" model in educative contexts and real therapy could indeed stand out as striking. In the ideal model, a main "theoretical" problem would be, for example, how to walk the line between giving one's partner too little or too much, whereas in the real therapies we observed the struggle turned out to be one of sharing interpretations of observed events (to the extent, of course, that the actors were capable of "observing" themselves).

Personal boundaries were highly relevant to the parent–child relationship too, particularly in the form of the concept of "attachment." "Attachment theory" has gained much attention across various fields in Norway over the last decade, and is in part inspired by various strands of psychotherapy, social work, and pedagogy in the United States. In the Family Therapy Unit at Modum, its presence is primarily through a socialization program called "COS", the Circle of Security Intervention (Powell et al. 2014). This program, which is presented for the patients at Modum in many forms—as a series of short educational videos, as a topic of discussion and reflection in larger groups, in the kindergarten and school, and in therapy—focuses on how children achieve autonomy through their own initiatives. The main point, as we understood it, is that such initiatives can only be taken as long as children feel secure. They gain this security from loving and encouraging parents who let their children explore their immediate environment, and who then are there to receive them as the children again seek the safety of the parents' embracing bodies. The circle of security gets larger as the children grow, but the basic logic stays the same. Clearly this philosophy made much sense to most parents we met at Modum Bad as it grasped in quite commonsense terms key ideals concerning nonintrusive and nonauthoritarian parenthood. "Attachment" appeared to them as a "natural" model of the ideal relationship and socialization process, a model that cultivates a sensitivity to the children's emerging integrity as it grows out of natural curiosity and a sense of being recognized and the subject of continuous interest. The egalitarian ethos seemed to appear as highly self-evident, as we never witnessed any attempt to formulate alternative models of authority. As such it illustrates our discussion of class above; although several patients were not used to this approach in their own socialization, or may not have applied it themselves as parents, they were clearly attracted to it and viewed it very positively. In more practical terms, dilemmas appeared here too, as the attachment theory did not imply inspiring children to ignore boundaries nor, it seemed, to lecture them explicitly about their precise nature. Rather, the message that was brought forth was one of implicit compassionate guidance, stimulating the child to gain experience from experimentation and to generalize from advice relating to that experimentation.

It is interesting to reflect on how ideas concerning "pure relationships" and the individual autonomy they seem to require are tied to more encompassing institutional arrangements and imaginaries. The sense of risk may be a useful case in point here. One important emergent property of the universally oriented Scandinavian welfare state is that it reconfigures ideas of personal risk. As risk is clearly one important reason why personal dependency appears attractive and necessary, "real" individual autonomy is strongly associated with social differentiation: class, gender, and ethnicity. The existence of a system of basic security and public services seems to, over time, inspire a sense of self that is less heavily influenced by fear of "falling from grace" or, more generally, of missing the opportunity of living a decent life (as conventionally defined) even when one loses one's job, gets divorced, fails at school, and so on. The point is very simple, and does not in any way need to involve the naïve assumption that class and gender differences are unimportant, but its implications have hardly been taken seriously enough. What I have in mind here is the strength of the seemingly widespread idea that such differences, although often tacitly acknowledged, do not undermine the possibility of acting as though individual autonomy is a paramount value, relevant for most people and in fact possible to realize. As a result, most arenas seem characterized by the relative absence of class- and gender-based sub-cultural identities, one important effect of which is that the overwhelm-ingly middle-class–influenced cultural values concerning what is seen as a good life are not seen as one cultural alternative among many. Very often it seems to pass as normal. This is what Henrik Stenius has in mind when discussing *The Good Life is a Life in Conformity* (1997), and what Jonas Frykman and Orvar Löfgren analyze in *Cultivated Man* (1979). Both these works, in turn, are wholly in line with John Barnes' acute obser-vations in Western Norway in the 1950s and with Marianne Gullestad's understanding of egalitarian individualism.

In the Scandinavian context, it has made a lot of sense to cultivate a worldview that makes it seem reasonable, for instance in the eyes of parents, to invest in young people's desire to become individually inde-pendent, even for girls/young women, and even among the working classes. This does not mean that opportunities are equal, but rather that (1) the majority seem to see this as both realistic and possible, and (2) that the risk of failing is normally not fatal in terms of becoming materi-ally miserable or being excluded from new chances. As I have pointed out above, this worldview is clearly based on the experience with welfare policy (family policy, education policy, labor market policy), but seems also to be embedded in a deeper institutional logic. In Scandinavia, the preference for some type of formal organization of social relations, per-haps particularly in close-knit communities where informal social con-trol was strong and was generalized quite early, had important effects on the conceptualization of trust. Formal organization was seen as a precondition for individual autonomy, and trusting others was to a great extent a question of evaluating people endowed with institutional responsibilities according to criteria drawn from the public sphere. As I have indicated above, it seems reasonable to interpret the principle of universalism as both culturally and logically connected to this phenom-enon. Extending equal rights and access even to potential free-riders served as a mechanism for integration, and brought people into the uni-verse of shared conventions (conformity) to which strong mechanisms of formal control were intimately tied. In this sense, Giddens' idea of "pure relationships" is interesting. It rests on people's ability to imagine not only some, but most, social relationships as something from which they may *withdraw* if they so prefer. As long as such a perspective is reasonably widely shared, other kinds of differences may not be all that relevant, and thus not necessarily threaten a sense of equality even in the presence of obvious differences.

The so-called "attachment theory" is an interesting case in point here (Meyer et al. 2013). During our fieldwork in the world of psychiatry and family therapy, this theoretical approach was certainly paramount, and my impression is that it plays an important role in many contexts relating to socialization and parenting more generally. Attachment theory emphasizes the "natural authority" of parents and the ideal that children's emotions are to be met on the children's own premises, without condemnation, but through acceptance and sympathetic assistance by parents in connecting emotions to language. "Dangerous" emotions should not be tabooed, but instead be understood and interpreted as a means for making sense of complex experience and for channeling them into a meaningful, self-reflexive vocabulary. As I understand it, attachment theory puts priority on egalitarian, open, and self-reflexive dialogue between partners who learn to respect each other through the mutual understanding they gradually build as they seek to link emotions and language, and more mundanely, doing things together with a sense of inner meaningfulness and reciprocity. Indeed, attachment theory may seem like a declaration of individual autonomy. In psychiatric contexts, as I have experienced them, this makes much sense because the major challenge among most patients (at Modum Psychiatric Clinic) is to deal with individual boundaries and make such boundaries natural, in the sense of being able to reject being invaded by others without becoming exhausted, isolated, and the like. As pointed out by, among others, Charles Lindholm (2007) and Robert Bellah et al. (1985), middle-class America is an interesting point here, because individual autonomy has such a strong position. Also, the American middle class represents a fascinating contrast to the Scandinavian, especially due to the seemingly much stronger emphasis on the family, its distinct values, and relations of authority. In the United States, the family, alongside images of the community, stands out as deeper, more important, and authentic than public relations dominating in politics, corporate culture, and contexts associated with the power of experts. Of course, its material significance is much more central to the future of children growing up. According to Lindholm, egalitarian relations and horizontal solidarity relate uneasily with cultural models of paternal authority drawn from family life.

NATURAL AUTHORITY OR POWER STRUGGLE?

In an interesting study of the role of attachment theory among middle-class mothers in the United States, *Power Struggles: The Paradoxes of Emotion and Control Among Child-Centered Mothers in the Privileged United States*, Diane Hoffman (2013) discusses some fascinating dilemmas in the way the theory is understood and applied. The New York mothers she interviewed perceived of the relationship between parents and children in part as a power struggle. This, according to Hoffman, reflects the widespread assumption that individuality consists of a strong competitive will that almost by necessity must generate conflict. For the mothers, the attachment orientation is attractive because it may help them teach the children how to deal with potentially conflict-generating emotions. One guiding idea is that the children are encouraged to express or show their feelings, so that their parents can validate them (and as such, recognize the child's sense of self) and demonstrate that they do not see them as dangerous, out of place, and so on. However, Hoffman's material shows that rather than validating these emotions, the mothers channel them into their own vocabulary, which is in turn more or less imposed on the child. In other words, what the mothers do is not to encourage the expression of spontaneous emotions, but rather to teach them which categories their emotions can be legitimately channeled into, and thus controlled. The validation does not so much concern the children's emotions as the adult, middle-class standard to which their mothers strive to conform. Hoffman argues that the intense struggle to try to fit the children's expressions into adult sensibilities and what the adult sees as legitimate emotions, acceptable forms of self-control, and the like, can be seen as resources the mothers can use in demonstrating their identity vis-à-vis their relevant others, an activity characterized by an intense struggle for achieving status as the best parent within the context of a highly differentiated class society. It generates an illusion of autonomy, but most fundamentally, perhaps, is the effect that children tend to internalize the knowledge of how to manipulate others.

Perhaps Hoffman is exaggerating, but as I see it, she at least points at an important cultural dilemma. In a society where the sense of being vulnerable is getting stronger, and where competition, manipulation, and personal dependency influence social relations in most domains, it is not necessarily reasonable to expect that children, if only they expose their inner feelings, will be recognized and their feelings serve as the building blocks for the construction of "pure" relationships characterized by intimacy and trust. What it takes for such a dynamic to be realized in practice is hard to know, but as I have emphasized above, one key indicator is whether people from different class backgrounds, when meeting each other in, for example, therapeutic contexts, in fact act as though it may. One important factor here is their sense of risk. If individual autonomy is not something that everyone associates with a zero-sum game in which only the most privileged win, but rather an essential aspect of being human and free (in the Scandinavian context, this would often mean "normal"), and the consequences of not being successful are fatal (in the sense of falling from grace), it may indeed serve as a basic element in a shared worldview and dealt with as an important *as if* component. At Modum, no one ignores the significance of class, but at the same time people from diverse class backgrounds seem to assume that neither class nor gender stands in the way of speaking meaningfully about individual autonomy.

How Institutions Think

In Chap. 3 I discussed how the political worldview and practical action among local politicians are shaped by the institutional context within which politics take place. In that case, universalism makes sense from a particular local point of view, and is seen as resting on certain preconditions, whereas from a more managerial perspective it appears illogical and unrealistic due to the pressure of seeking budget responsibility and ambition to achieve organizational control. The same was seen as holding true with regard to political identity and sense of responsibility. Once responsibility becomes removed from concrete social networks, it seems easy to relativize it and make it a function of the personal loyalty one has to administrative and political superiors.

At Modum Psychiatric Clinic, I observed a similar phenomenon, this time related to something slightly different, but yet quite similar: how service providers tend to think about principles of service provision according to whether the institutional context is somehow locally controlled and bounded. The case involved psychologists at Modum who publicly embraced a new public policy involving evidence-based service packages to psychiatric patients in order to increase efficiency and make services both more user oriented and more easily accessible. It appeared that these psychologists were representative of the view among the staff at the clinic, but the professional outlook they formulated was completely at odds with the view shared by most professionals working closer to municipal service provision. The distinctive contrast between the conditions under which these two actors work concerns the possibility to relate to preselected patients and thus how they would avoid becoming absorbed by capacity problems or, alternatively, actually become absorbed by them.

In Modum Psychiatric Clinic's own area there is another institution formally run by the clinic, but that provides services to other client groups under very different conditions, Modum District Psychiatric Center (DPS). It provides psychiatric services (advisory services, but mostly therapy) to the local population of Modum and two neighboring municipalities (Krødsherad and Sigdal). These patients apply for services with a government-issued guarantee in their hands. Within three weeks the DPS is obliged to respond to the applications (which are formulated and issued by municipal doctors or psychologists), and the threshold for rejecting applications is high. A prioritization guide, also issued by the government, is used as the guiding principle for selecting patients and establishing queues, and emphasizes treatment cost and realistic possibilities for healing along with some special guidelines for focusing on psychiatric problems deemed particularly important from the perspective of public health. During our fieldwork at Modum, our attention was drawn to this clinic as we realized that the professionals working there were seemingly distinctively different in several respects. We learned, first, that many among them were very critical of the therapeutic outlook of their colleagues at Modum Psychiatric Clinic. The latter tend to work according to evidence-based models, and according to our informants at the DPS the adherence to models seems "orthodox" at times. They felt that it prevents the use of professional discretion, and that it stimulates a tendency to follow therapeutic fads and enthusiastic support of professional stars who happened to able to market their models and manuals successfully. For such reasons, critical perspectives and discussions may become discouraged and even suppressed. They themselves argued that they felt their ability to provide adequate therapy depended on a broader knowledge of many different approaches and methods, mostly because the patients seeking treatment were so diverse. As they saw it, they adapted to the needs of the patients rather than imposing one standard model upon them.

As indicated above, this reflected a very different institutional reality between the two neighboring institutions. Modum Psychiatric Clinic selects a set number of patients from a very long queue, and to some extent, this privilege enables the institution to select patients that fit the models it offers. No such possibility exists in the DPS context. Because of this, some of the staff questioned the political priorities behind this striking difference, indicating that Modum Psychiatric Clinic was in a privileged position compared to municipal services. As the staff at the DPS experienced their world, they faced an almost overwhelming demand that could not be meaningfully handled in terms of the prioritization guidelines. Thus in practice they tried to treat as many patients as possible, and distribute the available resources as evenly and justly as possible. As they saw it, their greatest asset in this situation was their ability to adapt flexibly to the needs of very diverse patients, and be able to apply a variety of psychotherapeutic approaches. In their eyes, standardization coupled with state-issued guarantees to users would increase their dilemma, because it would undermine their ability to be sensitive and adaptable. Also, it would most probably hinder them from making priorities that from a local point of view looked reasonable, given their extended knowledge of what patients need. In addition to this, they voiced a deep scepticism to rigorous evidence-based methods as the means for selecting and privileging treatment methods. The main reason for this was not based on some psychotherapeutic ideology, but was pragmatic. Because in reality there are few possibilities to reproduce the conditions existing in ideal test situations (from which evidence is inferred), applying them means performing a mechanical, and even flawed, form of therapy, alienating the therapist from her or his expertise and experience, as well as alienating therapist and patient from each other.

As we experienced the two neighboring institutions, the working conditions were strikingly different. The staff at the DPS was to a great extent caught between state guarantees and guidelines and the need to protect themselves from becoming completely overwhelmed by the demand, while trying to provide quality treatment. However, the staff at Modum Psychiatric Clinic was "protected" by their ability to admit a certain number of patients and thus secure highly predictive working conditions. The latter were not directly affected by, or concerned with, those who were not admitted (for the staff at Modum Psychiatric Clinic, that naturally appears as a political problem), whereas the former constantly had to deal with that challenge. Because of this, they came to see their world very differently, including what is supposed to count as good therapy. This difference was publicly expressed in a debate in the national newspaper *Morgenbladet* in the fall of 2015, some six months after our fieldwork. It was triggered by a government proposal to introduce standardized therapeutic packages, so that patients would get more adequate treatment faster, and have access to a prepared path through the treatment system. In one specific issue of *Morgenbladet*, two research psychologists at Modum Psychiatric Clinic argued in favor of it, and another psychologist who leads a unit structurally similar to the DPS at Modum, argued against it. However, the structural conditions determining their points of view remained implicit. As I saw it, the two approaches both seemed perfectly sensible, but did not enter a dialogue and did not address the overall question: how to devise health policies that are adaptable to diverse institutional environments, and how to perform professional therapy and interpret methodology, science, and evidence in contextually sensitive ways.

Here's an excerpt of the argument presented by the two psychologists at Modum Psychiatric Clinic:

> There is ... no contradiction between close and nourishing cooperation and the use of specific models.
>
> The ... cognitive model for treating social phobia is well documented empirically. In one study done at Modum Psychiatric Clinic we found that changes in perpetuating processes in the first half of the treatment period predicted changed in social anxiety in the second. The effect was robust. Taken together the estimated processes explained most changes in anxiety. Therefore, it is reasonable to assume that these processes were present among the majority of the participants in the study. In a more comprehensive study of this cognitive model and psychodynamic therapy, more patients got rid of the anxiety through cognitive therapy. In other words, different treatment methods produced different outcome.
>
> The preconditions for incorporating the cognitive model in a treatment path package are ... present. In such a treatment path package the therapist may quickly identify the perpetuating processes present in social phobia that otherwise are difficult to discover. Also, research findings enable the therapists to inform the patient about the chance of healing.

Psychotherapeutic research support[s] the use of treatment path packages, precisely because parts of the basis for treatment consist of testing different packages or specific treatment methods against each other. However, it is a problem that these packages are not used in normal clinical practice to any significant degree. The introduction of treatment path packages may contribute to increasing the implementation. (Asle Hoffart and Sverre Urnes Johnson in *Morgenbladet*, October 9, 2015)

The alternative approach was formulated in the following terms, authored by the leader of Stangehjelpa, a municipal psychiatric institution in the municipality of Stange, Southeast Norway.

In Stangehjelpa, which I lead, we are primarily concerned with the human sciences – culture, because that is the focus among those we are here to help. Therefore, we work on the basis of principles rather than manuals. We carefully audit our results rather than blindly following procedures or treatment paths. And our results are so good that we are often asked to present our work at conferences, we receive interested visitors from other municipalities, and contribute wherever we can to further develop the field. But it is not easy to standardize what we are doing, and this creates problems for politicians who would like to control the variation in service provision. Then, one turns to a simpler solution – within the parameters of the natural sciences – culture, a standardized treatment path delivered in the form of a package. If Stangehjelpa was to be incorporated under a treatment path package regime, it would die. (Birgit Valla in *Morgenbladet*, September 25, 2015)

As I see it, both may be perfectly right. At least, the arguments make perfect sense when taking into consideration the institutional context from which they speak. During our fieldwork at Modum Psychiatric Clinic, we learned that the sometimes very rhetorical emphasis on evidence-based psychiatry in the sense described by Hoffart and Johnsen is somewhat controversial. In the case described above, drawn from family therapy, most Norwegian therapists and treatment methods have been firmly established in "the human sciences—culture." (Valla 2015) However, at Modum such approaches are used together with more evidence-based models and methods, seemingly without much dispute. My point here is a very simple one. Modum Psychiatric Clinic, which is a very successful and renowned institution, is institutionally well equipped to pursue professional ideals and methods that are simply unrealistic and potentially destructive in other institutional contexts. Thus the question is not whether the two actors in this case have it right or wrong in terms of the philosophy of science, but rather what institutional context makes it possible to enact certain truths and mobilize interests (political, bureaucratic, professional) behind such truths. Two implications seem particularly interesting. First, as outlined in Chap. 3 in particular, universalism, here understood pragmatically as an institutionally backed ambition and pressure to provide services to people who could easily be ignored by those whose concern is to protect budgets and institutional boundaries, is simply unimaginable without some sort of institutional autonomy. Modum Psychiatric Hospital illustrates such an autonomy, but in a somewhat unconventional way. In contrast to municipalities, it provides services under conditions that are almost perfectly controlled. Because of this, it becomes possible to focus intensely on service quality and even cultivate the view that there is no contradiction whatsoever among standardization, service demand, and quality. Municipalities, on the other hand, and much like the Modum DPS, are under a heavy pressure to meet an overwhelming demand, and politicians, bureaucrats, and service providers have, over time, become experts in lowering standards of quality according to the pressure to distribute resources as evenly as possible to an increasing number of users.

CONCLUSION

As pointed out in Chap. 1, I think that Mary Douglas' view of how institutions think is, at least in part, very simplistic. Institutions do not automatically transform problems into solutions that fit "the limited range of their experience" (Douglas 1986: 92), nor do they "channel our perceptions into forms compatible with the relations they authorize" (ibid.). At the very least, institutions are areas of conflicting interests and contestation, and their "output" consists of much more messiness than allowed for by Douglas' perspective. In addition, it is no doubt often not at all in harmony with "what they authorize." This, in my view, is one major reason why we should in fact study them ethnographically both from within and outside. My main point in this chapter has been to show that institutional contexts provide powerful affordances, and provide cultural models that are not only good to think with, but which become "real" because they appear realistically attached to available paths of action that allow certain interests to be realized (at the cost of others; Kronenfeld 2008; Vike 2012). Such affordances may have a profound influence of

highly different social phenomena such as the construction of person-
hood, ontological ideas of what constitutes social relationships, scientific
truth, policy models, and institutional boundaries.

REFERENCES

Barnes, J. 1954. Class and Committees in a Norwegian Island Parish. *Human Relations* 7 (1): 39–58.
Beck, Ulrich. 2002. *Individualization: Institutionalized Individualism and Its Social and Political Consequences*. London: Sage.
Bellah, Robert N., et al. 1985. *Habits of the Heart: Commitment and Individualism in American Life*. Berkeley: University of California Press.
Berger, Peter, et al. 1974. *The Homeless Mind: Modernization and Consciousness*. New York: Vintage Books.
Collins, Randall. 2011. Patrimonial Alliances and Failures of State Penetration: A Historical Dynamic of Crime. Corruption, Gangs, and Mafias. *The Annals of the American Academy of Political and Social Sciences*, 636, June: 16–31.
Douglas, Mary. 1986. *How Institutions Think*. New York: Syracuse University Press.
Frykman, Jonas, and Orvar Löfgren. 1979. *Den kultiverade människan*. Lund: Liber forlag.
Giddens, Anthony. 1991. *Modernity and Self-Identity: Self and Society in the Late Modern Age*. Cambridge: Polity Press.
Gullestad, Marianne. 1992. Symbolic Fences. In *The Art of Social Relations. Essays on Culture, Social Action and Everyday Life in Modern Norway*. Oslo: Scandinavian University Press.
Hoffman, Diane M. 2013. Power Struggles: The Paradoxes of Emotion and Control among Child-Centered Mothers in Privileged United States. *Ethos* 41 (1): 75–97.
Hoffart, Asle and Sverre Urnes Johnsen. 2015. *Bedre med pakkeforløp enn selvstandardisering*. Oslo: Morgenbladet (Sept. 25).
Kronenfeld, David B. 2008. *Culture, Society, and Cognition: Collective Goals, Values, Action, and Knowledge*. New York: Mouton de Gruyter.
Lindholm, Charles. 2007. *Culture and Identity: The History, Theory and Practice of Psychological Anthropology*. Oxford: Oneworld Publications.
Löfgren, Orvar. 1987. Deconstructing Swedisness: Culture and Class in Modern Sweden. In *Anthropology at Home*, ed. Jackson, Anthony, 74–93. ASA Monographs 25. London: Tavistock Publications.
Meyer, Dixie, Wood Sarah, and Stanley Bethany 2013. *The Family Journal*, 21 (2): 162–169.

Powell, Bert, and Charles H. Zeanah. 2014. *The Circle of Security Intervention Enhancing Attachment in Early Parent-Child Relationships*. New York: Guilford Press.

Sørensen, Øystein, and Bo Stråth. 1997. *The Cultural Construction of Norden*. Oslo: Scandinavian University Press.

Stenius, Henrik. 2010. Nordic Associational Life in a European and an Inter-Nordic Perspective. In *Nordic Associations in a European Perspective*, ed. Henrik Stenius and Risto Alapuro. Nomos: Baden-Baden.

Tilly, Charles. 1990. *Coercion, Capital and European States, A.D. 990-1990*. New York: Cambridge University Press.

Tilly, Charles. 2004. *Contention & Democracy in Europe, 1650-2000*. Cambridge: Cambridge University Press.

Trägårdh, Lars. 1997. Statist Individualism. On the Culturality of the Nordic Welfare State. In *The Cultural Construction of Norden*, eds. Sørensen, Øystein and Bo Stråth, 253–285. Oslo: Scandinavian University Press.

Trägårdh, Lars. 2008. Det civila samhällets karriär som vetenskapligt och politiskt begrepp i Sverige. *Tidskrift för samfunnsforskning* 49 (4): 575–594.

Valla, Birgit. 2015. *Det er greit å ta feil*. Oslo: Morgenbladet (Sept. 25).

Vike, Halvard. 2012. Varianter av vest-europeiske statsformasjoner–Utkast til en historisk antropologi. *Norsk antropologisk tidsskrift* 23 (2): 126–142.

Weinstein, Deborah. 2013. *Pathological Family: Cold War America and the Rise of Family Therapy*. New York: Cornell University Press.

CHAPTER 9

Conclusions

POLITICAL MOBILIZATION AND STATE FORMATION IN SCANDINAVIA: THE STRENGTHS OF HORIZONTAL TIES

As an ethnographer of politics and bureaucracy, I find myself wondering why the study of the formal institutions of "the state" is so fragmented and why, in my view, the underlying dynamics of institutional forms seem so poorly understood. Although it is common among my informants to talk about institutions as though they were things that are supposed to work as tools for some higher political and managerial intention, and thus in a sense directly comparable with (or actually derived from) the cognitive models they use to represent institutional forms symbolically most informants seem to know very well that they have to act according to very different and more pragmatic understandings. This seems not necessarily to be the case with analysts, policy makers, and managers, who tend to stick more consistently to their own reifications. Provided that this observation has some validity, the reason why models seem to blend in with the realities they are supposed to represent may be very simple. We, as humans, talk about the patterns we observe as though they were more or less stable entities with a capacity to act according to some intention, all or most of the time. Anthropologist David Kronenfeld, in *Culture, Society,*

© The Author(s) 2018   177
H. Vike, *Politics and Bureaucracy in the Norwegian Welfare State,*
Approaches to Social Inequality and Difference,
https://doi.org/10.1007/978-3-319-64137-9_9

and Cognition: Collective Goals, Values, Action, and Knowledge (2008), indeed argues that this capacity may have been what has led anthropologists to cultivate a somewhat reified concept of culture.

In political science and sociology, there seems to have developed a sense of urgency concerning the felt need to revise our understanding of institutions based on methods that are more sensitive. This may help us build models on observed social relations and processes rather than abstract models that tend to import more or less implicit normative standards of how we ought to organize our world and control it. In anthropology, "the state" and its institutions remain an elusive category, and to date there is a very strong tendency to concentrate on the margins and on how people around the world imagine it. My attempt to access it by moving in and out of institutions is an attempt to offer an approach that may inspire others to explore formal institutions, politics, power, bureaucracy, and so on through the eyes, representations, interests, actions, and social relationships of those who enact the state on a daily basis.

To my mind, comparative theories of state formation emerging from political science and historical sociology have a lot to offer such an ambition. Charles Tilly's work, among others, has made it very clear that in Europe, the variation is great and much remains unexplained. The Northern European periphery, for example, which has been my focus in the present book, may represent a more fascinating historical trajectory that what is usually assumed. Why did the universally oriented welfare state emerge in the first place, and why has it survived? How can it be that notions and ideals of individual autonomy loom so large within a political order that is more thoroughly bureaucratized than, perhaps, any other democratic state on the globe? Why haven't neoliberal movements such as those associated with The Third Way and "The Blair Supremacy," privatization, and managerial authoritarianism succeeded in appropriating institutions and undermined the possibility to exert popular influence?

In this book, I have made attempts to introduce a historical perspective along with my own ethnographic descriptions of contemporary local politics and bureaucratic work to address such questions better. One insight that has emerged is that there seem to exist some interesting links between the apparently often unacknowledged significance of early capitalism in Scandinavia, on the one hand, and state rule and political mobilization. The penetration of merchant and protoindustrial capitalism was indeed very thorough and took place at an early stage, but the resources it generated were much less subject to monopolist control than in the rest of Europe. Peasant-farmers were brought into close interaction with state rulers partly because of this, and entered a field of political contention where their political influence became significant, partly because landlordism was relatively marginal (and in Norway almost nonexistent). Consequently, local forms of cooperation, political participation, and mobilization gained ground and served as useful mechanisms for dealing with state rulers, who on their part could introduce and gradually strengthen state control through institutions that to a significant extent constituted extensions of such forms. In sum, the institutionalization of political participation was characterized by a significant continuity. Moreover, in the long run it contributed much to transcending the "worst" forms of class conflict, as political mobilization in part had a uniting effect, reinforced by the redistributive ambitions that class compromises made possible and which were translated into state policy. Finally, the specific forms political participation took in Scandinavia deeply affected popular ideas of the collective good as something delegated to the state, and benefiting broad sections of the population.

In this book I have been concerned not only with the emergence of the modern state and the political culture of which it is a part, but also the reproduction of both. In this light, the question "why has the welfare state survived" may appear somewhat awkward. However, my point is this: we need to focus on how political orders/systems are in fact reproduced, and in order to do that it is not enough to map aggregate patterns, models, norms, representations, and the like, but look more systematically at social relationships, processes and patterns that generate them and emerge from them. As concerns the Scandinavian welfare state, the assumption that Scandinavians are characterized by a certain cultural naïveté concerning what a strong state really is and is capable of doing in terms of undermining freedom, is deeply unsatisfying. The same goes for the belief that there exists a particular "culture of consensus" in the region, as well as the hypothesis that some type of "social democratic hegemony" provides an ideological template for "state friendliness" and state paternalism. Small size cannot explain very much either, nor can the idea that in Scandinavia there has been so much money around that austerity has not yet become as urgent as in the rest of Europe.

As I see it, this line of reasoning calls for an institutional perspective on political culture and state formation. To repeat: claims to cultural specificity explain very little in terms of why and how the political order in contemporary Scandinavia emerged in the form it did. In this book I have tried to illuminate some aspects of how institutions work, and I have tried to show that their dynamic is quite deeply influenced by some specific qualities of the social relations among those who take part in them. Political participation in Norway is strongly shaped by voluntary membership and, as I have argued, *the morality of membership* seems to constitute a major social experience and a powerful metaphor. This has provided people who otherwise have a hard time competing for attractive resources on an individual basis with a template for collective action and horizontal alliances. I have tried to show that these forms, at least under some circumstances, may be powerful enough to challenge hierarchically organized power, as well as, in recent times, to resist the influence of neoclientelist forms of personal loyalty that are reintroduced through managerial governance. In Chap. 1 in particular, I discussed the morality of membership in terms of Mauss' classic analysis of the gift. This analytical metaphor served useful, I hope, in illuminating how horizontal alliances are reproduced through morally controlled forms of value circulation. Mutual trust, social control, representation, and commitment are valuable resources that need to be managed collectively as collective goods, and this control is achieved largely through a type of conformity that, in functional terms, seems useful as a means for preventing mutual horizontal commitment from being "invaded" by claims to individual loyalty based on bureaucratic-managerial criteria. This contrasts with the gift-giving dynamics described by Mauss, however, in the sense that any gift between people who deal with each other as equals (qua members) may be rejected, terminated, or annulled by exit. In other words, the gift-giving logic made possible by the morality of membership (described here as an "ideal type" in Weber's terms) is not only one of the obligation to give, receive, and reciprocate, but also everyone's moral right to negotiate the terms, reject, or exit. Moreover, throughout the book I have tried to demonstrate that the relative power of horizontal alliances to influence policy and institutions is in part due to their capability to mobilize across institutional boundaries. This is one reason, I also argue, that the notion of "civil society" as a separate domain beyond the state, characterized by a set of different norms, values, relationships, and capabilities, seemingly makes less sense in Scandinavia than in, say the United States.

Several recent developments in social theory have contributed much to renewing our perspective on conventional analytical dichotomies such as that separating "modern" from "traditional." However, this dichotomy lingers on and has a profound influence on both popular and scientific models of historical change and contemporary society. If democracy, individualism, universalism, human rights, and so on are not phenomena emerging from modernism and the specific transformations related to the development of capitalism, bureaucracy, and the emergence of mass politics, then how can they be understood? What seems clear is that although there is no such thing as a single modernity, nor some evolutionary logic according to which historical change leads to "more" modern forms, we seem stuck with a sense that human rights, for example, are (or should be) a universal value, and that in order to realize them, some particular institutional structure and a specific set of rationalities and competencies are indeed needed.

Throughout the chapters of this book, I have tried to show that the path towards what we may reasonably label "egalitarian democracy" and "welfare state" is not one of progressive modernity emerging from the institutional centers of "the state." Democracy clearly depends on the relative success of political mobilization from below, as well as the ability to prevent powerful institutions and the elites that are supposed to control them from becoming autonomous. In Norway, the horizontal alliances established through political resistance and contention have had a fundamental role to play in undermining and marginalizing not only forms of power related to premodern social orders, such as clientelism, particularism, privilege, and authoritarianism, they have also been important in preventing such forms from being reintroduced and dominant in new contexts and new disguises. At the same time as "modernization" is endowed with the status as the paramount symbol of the measures taken to establish new forms of control over institutions from the top down, personal loyalty and what I have called "neoclientelism," particularism (e.g., in the form of conditionality and selectivism in service provision), authoritarian control, "retraditionalization" of women and female-dominated service provision, and elite autonomy are reintroduced. This is one reason why I have stressed the principle of universalism in this anthropological approach to politics and bureaucracy. As one of the prototypical symbols of modernity, universalism serves to highlight one of my main points. It seems unthinkable that universalism (at least in the form of universal service provision) can survive without institutions that are profoundly influenced by popular forms of political resistance capable of preventing political and administrative institutional elites who, as a part of their pursuit of controlling institutions more effectively, are likely to fight any principle and measure that fundamentally undermines such control.

REFERENCE

Kronenfeld, David B. 2008. *Culture, Society, and Cognition. Collective Goals, Values, Action, and Knowledge*. Berlin: Mouton de Gruyter.

BIBLIOGRAPHY

Alexander, Jeffrey C. 2006. *The Civil Sphere*. New York/Oxford: University of Oxford Press.

Bakken, Runar. 2004. *Mann i ingenmannsland. Om menn i omsorg, hjemme og ute*. Bergen: Fagbokforlaget.

Baldersheim, Harald and Lawrence E. Rose (eds.) 2000. *Det kommunale laboratorium. Teoretiske perspektiver på kommunal organisering*. Bergen: Fagbokforlaget.

Barth, Fredrik. 1987. *Cosmologies in the Making: A Generative Approach to Cultural Variation in Inner New Guinea*. Cambridge: Cambridge University Press.

Barth, Erling et al. 2014. The Scandinavian Model—An Interpretation. *The Journal of Public Economics* 127: 17–29.

Bendixen, Synnøve, Mary-Bente Bringslid, and Halvard Vike. (eds.). 2017. *Egalitarianism in Scandinavia. Historical and Contemporary Perspectives*. New York: Palgrave MacMillan.

Blom, Ida. 2016. Troubled and Secure Gender Identities in a Changing Society: Norway at the End of the Long Nineteenth Century. In *Gendered Citizenship: The Politics of Representation*, ed. Hilde Danielsen, Kari Jegerstedt, Ragnhild Muriaas, and Brita Ytre-Arne, 37–60. London: Palgrave Macmillan.

Bom-Hansen, Jens. 2010. Municipal Amalgamations and Common Pool Problems: The Danish Local Government Reform in 2007. *Scandinavian Political Studies* 33 (1): 51–73.

Briseid, Kristin M. 2017. *On the Old and the New. An Ethnographic Study of Older People's Mental Health Services in a Changing Welfare State*. PhD Thesis, Drammen: University College of Southeast Norway.

Bruun, Maja Hojer et al. (eds.). 2011. Introduction: The Concern for Sociality-Practicing Equality and Hierarchy in Denmark. *Social Analysis* 55 (2): 1–19.
Bryden, John, et al. 2015. *Northern Neighbours: Scotland and Norway Since 1800.* Edinburgh: Edinburgh University Press.
Dahl, Hans Fredrik. 1986. Those Equal Folk. In *Norden: The Passion for Equality*, ed. S.R. Graubard, 97–112. Oslo: Norwegian University Press.
Esping-Andersen, Gösta. 2005. Inequality of Incomes and Opportunities. In *The New Egalitarianism*, ed. Anthony Giddens, and Patrick Diamond, 8–39. Cambridge and Malden: Polity Press.
Esping-Andersen, Gösta. 2009. *The Incomplete Revolution. Adapting to Women's New Roles.* Cambridge: Polity Press.
Etzioni, Amitai. 1995. *The Spirit of Community Rights, Responsibilities and the Communitarian Agenda.* London: Fontana Press.
Fukuyama, Francis. 1995. *Trust. The Social Virtues and the Creation of Prosperity.* New York: Simon & Schuster.
Granberg, Mikael. 2008. Local Governance "in Swedish"? Globalisation, Local Welfare and Beyond. *Local Government Studies* 34 (1): 363–377.
Gullestad, Marianne. 1984. *Kitchen-Table Society. A Case Study of the Family Life and Friendships of Young Working-Class Mothers in Urban Norway.* Oslo: Universitetsforlaget.
Gullestad, Marianne. 2001. Likhetens grenser. In *Likhetens paradokser. Antropologiske undersøkelser i det moderne Norge*, ed. Marianne E. Lien, Hilde Lidén, and Halvard Vike. Oslo: Universitetsforlaget.
Gullestad, Marianne. 2002. Invisible Fences: Egalitarianism, Nationalism and Racism. *Journal of the Royal Anthropological Institute* 8 (1): 199–226.
Grimen, H. 2009. *Hva er tillit?.* Oslo: Universitetsforlaget.
Holtedahl, Lisbeth 1994. *Hva mutter gjør er alltid viktig. Om å være kvinne og mann i en nordnorsk bygd i 1970-årene.* Oslo: Universitetsforlaget.
Jenkins, Richard. 2011. *Being Danish. Paradoxes of Identity in Everyday Life.* Copenhagen: Museum Tusculanum Press.
Kaspersen, Lars B., and Laila Ottesen. 2001. Associationalism for 150 Years and Still Alive and Kicking: Some Reflections on Danish Civil Society. *Critical Review of International and Political Philosophy* 4 (1): 105–130.
Knudsen, Tim. 2002. Den nordiske velferdsstat og de sekulariserede luthera-nere. In *Velferd og folkeoplysning*, ed. Søren Eigaard, 11–29. Odense: Odense Universitetsforlag.
Lien, Marianne E., Hilde Lidén, and Halvard Vike (eds.). 2001. *Likhetens paradokser. Antropologiske undersøkelser i det moderne Norge.* Oslo: Universitetsforlaget.
Mauss, Marcel. 2000. *The Gift: The Form and Reason for Exchange in Archaic Societies.* New York: WW Norton & Company.

Pierre, Jon, and Bo Rothstein. (eds.). 2003. *Välfärdsstat i otakt. Om politikens oväntade, oavsiktliga och oönskade effekter*. Lund: Liber.

Seip, Anne Lise. 1992. *Velferdsstatens utvikling. Trangen til trygghet og en ny rasjonalitet*. Ad Notam: Oslo.

Sainsbury, Diane. 1999. *Gender and Welfare State Regimes*. Oxford: Oxford University Press.

Sørhaug, Hans Christian. 1986. Totemisme på norsk – betraktninger om det norske sosialdemokratiets vesen. In *Den norske væremåten*, ed. Arne Martin Klausen, 61–88. Oslo: Da Capo.

Tranvik, Tommy and Per Selle. 2007. More Centralization, Less Democracy: The Decline of the Democratic Infrastructure in Norway. In *State and Civil Society in Northern Europe. The Swedish Model reconsidered*, ed. Trägårdh, Lars, 205–229. New York and Oxford: Berghahn Books.

Vike, Halvard. 2011. Cultural Models, Power, and Hegemony. In *A Companion to Cognitive Anthropology*, ed. Kronenfeld, David B. et al., 376–393. Chichester: Wiley-Blackwell.

Vike, Halvard. 2013. Utopian Time and Contemporary Time: Temporal Dimensions of Planning and Reform in the Norwegian Welfare State. In *Elusive Promises. Planning in the Contemporary World*, ed. Abram, Simone and Weszkalnys, 35–57. New York: Oxford: Berghahn Books.

Vohnsen, Nina H. 2017. *The Absurdity of Bureaucracy*. UK: Oxford University Press.

INDEX

The manufacturer's authorised representative in the EU is Springer
Nature Customer Service Centre GmbH, Europaplatz 3, 69115 Heidelberg,
Germany. If you have any concerns regarding our products, please
contact ProductSafety@springernature.com

Printed and bound by CPI Group (UK) Ltd, Croydon, CR0 4YY
02/05/2026
02101650-0001